12⁵⁰

The
Duck
Hunter's
Handbook

The Duck Hunter's Handbook

Bob Hinman

Winchester Press

WINCHESTER is a Trademark of Olin Corporation
used by Winchester Press, Inc. under authority
and control of the Trademark Proprietor.

Third printing   1977

Copyright © 1974 by Bob Hinman
All rights reserved

Library of Congress Catalog Card Number: 74-78700
ISBN: 0-87691-146-7

WINCHESTER PRESS
205 East 42nd Street
New York, N.Y. 10017

This book is dedicated to members
of the Twin Springs Duck Club.

Acknowledgments

I want to thank Frank C. Bellrose, of the Illinois Natural History Survey, for consultation and allowing use of the migration corridor maps as well as other statistical material; wildlife artist Bruce Matteson, for the cover painting done in his unique style of montage; *Shooting Times* magazine, for allowing me to excerpt parts of previous articles; and, as always, Marilyn Owen, whose research, typing, and juggling of words keeps the author in print.

Contents

Introduction

N orth America possesses more waterfowl than any other
continent. Small wonder, then, that a rich tradition of
waterfowling has developed in our country. Originally, of course,
the activity was purely functional. Among the Indians, and later
among the early settlers, wildfowling was primarily a means of
putting food in the pot. However, about a century ago the hunting of ducks and geese began to be regarded as a sport or a
leisure activity rather than merely a means of providing meat
for the table. By 1900 the sport of waterfowling had grown to
such an extent that a considerable sporting literature existed in
which accounts of memorable hunts, explanations of various
methods of hunting waterfowl, and descriptions of the appearance
and habits of the principal duck species were set forth in elabo-
rate detail for the edification of multitudes of avid sportsmen.

Waterfowling has changed a great deal since those days—partly
in good ways, partly in bad. Duck populations have exhibited a
slow but steady decline as agriculture and other manifestations
of civilization have usurped or degraded millions of acres of the
sloughs and marshes needed to support their existence. However,
this slow deterioration has been, and is being, ameliorated somewhat as hunters provide funds to state and federal agencies, as

well as Ducks Unlimited, for the purpose of acquiring, restoring, and developing needed wetlands.

In contrast to the duck population there are probably more geese in North America now than when Columbus landed. For while the heartland of duck production, the northern prairies, has proved vulnerable to agricultural exploitation, most geese breed in the arctic and subarctic. Their breeding grounds are almost as untouched by man today as they were a hundred years ago. Moreover, a warming climatic trend in recent decades has favored successful nesting by arctic geese, and even more important, perhaps, geese have proved highly susceptible to management on wintering grounds.

Ducks do much of their feeding in the water, but nature adapted geese to feed primarily on land, and their food requirements are favorably associated with agriculture. Game biologists recognized a couple of decades ago that producing food crops for geese and regulating their kill could result in sizable increases in their numbers. Hence, in the past twenty years we have witnessed a steady expansion in lands acquired by conservation agencies for the purpose of growing crops for geese. Such increased food supply and adequate husbandry have resulted in five to six million geese visiting the United States each fall and winter.

Though this flourishing goose population is fine for those seeking geese, the fact remains that most waterfowlers hunt ducks. Not only are ducks closer to many hunters' doorsteps, but most wildfowlers prefer the trickier targets ducks provide, and especially the way in which they are hunted. For to view the sun coming up over a duck marsh and to see the marsh come to life is incomparable, a thrill unequaled anywhere. Dawn in a duck blind is simply something else compared with views of agricultural lands, lovely though they can be.

This may partly explain duck hunting's singular mystique, and the fact that although ducks have declined during the past century, interest in duck hunting has not. Over three times as many people purchase duck stamps today as in 1934 when they were first issued, even though the rules of duck hunting have been tightened almost annually, and with each new restriction many hunters vow to hang up their guns forever. For most complainers the "forever" only lasts until the next fall, while those who do abandon the sport are replaced by neophytes.

The days when a man could kill as many as a thousand ducks in a single season are long gone, but the essence of the sport remains. By and large, most hunters have understandingly accepted the restrictions on high kills. There is a new breed of waterfowler today. More and more of them seek only the opportunity to sit in a blind, watch the pageantry of flocks trading back and forth, match their calling ability against the sagacity of a wild duck, and perhaps with luck bag at least part of a limit. So today's waterfowler doesn't need to kill as many ducks as did the old-timers to feel he has accomplished his mission.

By the same token, of course, the hunter newly recruited to waterfowling can hardly be expected to match the skills of the old-timers, the men who made a profession of killing waterfowl for the market. Prior to World War I, these professionals were in the field almost every day from early September through April. They learned to know their quarry intimately, and where and when to hunt. They knew how to entice the birds and they became crack shots. Almost equaling their skills were the wealthy business and professional people who could afford to hunt for days on end and often employed market hunters as their guides.

Today, the average waterfowler hunts only about six and one-half days a year, and this limited time afield does not afford sufficient opportunity to develop the subtle skills so essential to good hunting. Consequently, untold thousands are more or less ignorant of certain basic facts about the sport they pursue. As I look down from the plane on flights over blinds in the Illinois and Mississippi River valleys, I see many blunders that hunters make: spreads of decoys that bear no resemblance to live ducks; blinds that reveal all too clearly the hunters within, or which appear utterly incongruous with the landscape; and boats and motors that stand out like sore thumbs. Most of these faults result, of course, from lack of knowledge and experience.

One of life's great pleasures is the anticipation of an upcoming pleasure, and waterfowlers are notorious for the eagerness with which they await the next season. Months beforehand they clean and reoil their guns, touch up decoys, paint duck boats, patch boots; and weeks before the season starts, they build blinds. Another excellent way to prepare for the coming season is to acquire more knowledge, and the best way I know is through books. The sportsman can do much vicariously to make up for his limited opportunities in the field if he will spend some time reading books about his sport that are instructive as well as entertaining.

This is just such a book. In convenient handbook format, Bob Hinman offers advice that should help any waterfowler achieve better hunting. He grew up shooting with old-timers who passed on to him by word and deed much that they had learned from long experience; and Bob went on to adapt his hunting techniques to modern guns, shotshells, and competition from "the guy in the next blind." Here you will find many practical suggestions for solving modern hunting problems and acquiring the skills needed for a more productive day in the blind.

Frank C. Bellrose
Illinois Natural History Survey
Havana, Illinois
March 1974

Author's Foreword

O ne of the milder annoyances the novice wildfowler must endure, as part of his initiation into duck hunting, is the endless talk about the "old days" when the skies were black with ducks. The new man will be told that all the good shooting is gone, and that it's hardly worth the effort to set out decoys these days. Of course the complainer himself is usually still hunting, even though he heard the same story when he was a boy.

Sure, the world will never again see the likes of America's "golden age" of duck hunting, which spanned some fifty years prior to World War I. But in spite of today's short seasons and small bags, duck hunting does have a future, and hunters will be on the marsh each fall as long as there is a season to hunt. There will always be new hunters among us to share our knowledge and tradition as well as something of the indescribable joy of just being there.

No one has given a completely satisfactory explanation of why men hunt, because it is compounded of so many different elements. When done under the rules of good sportsmanship, duck hunting is a culmination of art, skill, and scientific endeavor. It is also an act of love, for who loves the birds more than the hunter?

The hunter is not a breed apart, nor the wildfowler a distinct species; but hunting is a way of life, and my own would have been infinitely poorer without it. No one ever forgets his first sunrise on the marsh, or the first duck he takes cleanly on the wing. Such pleasures do not lessen with age or repetition, and neither does the delightful agony of waiting for each coming season.

It's only fair to warn the beginner that duck hunting can also mean long hours of hard, dirty, and sometimes dangerous work, done in foul weather under wretched conditions. It is a dedicated calling answered at the risk of economic and social advancement as well as marital tranquillity. For if waterfowling is more fascinating and compelling than other forms of hunting, it is also more demanding. The conditions under which waterfowl are hunted are more varied, and require more specialized equipment and more skill in using it than are needed for any other type of hunting. Fortunately, this variety also affords the duck hunter a wide latitude of choice, and he can bite off what he wants to chew. A single season's dues for some duck clubs could buy a fullblown African safari, but equally fine shooting often exists on a public hunting area only a mile or two away for a fee of a few dollars per day.

The beginner is not required to be an expert in all phases of duck hunting, although many will eventually head toward that end. However, he will find it necessary to have some practical knowledge of the sport and the use of the equipment it involves for his hunt to reach a successful conclusion.

This handbook cannot promise to turn anyone into a master duck hunter overnight—only years of experience will achieve that, for the sport demands much judgment and much practice, and no advice can apply with equal validity to all types of hunting and all conditions. Nonetheless, I've tried to set down in these pages enough working instructions and practical advice to get the novice started, and I hope even to provide the veteran with a few new wrinkles and some entertaining reading about his favorite sport.

Bob Hinman
Peoria, Illinois

The
Duck
Hunter's
Handbook

I·
What Kind of Duck Is That ?

There are so many different facets to duck hunting that it's difficult to decide which one to start with. But one thing is certain: if you're going to hunt ducks, you'd better know what you're hunting for. Far too many hunters, even some of long experience, have only a spotty understanding of how to distinguish between the various species of waterfowl, whether on the wing or in the hand. Identifying ducks on the wing is tough for anyone, though this chapter will give you some of the tips the experts rely on. However, an inability to identify ducks in hand or close to is inexcusable, and in this day and age in which an increasing number of states apply a point system in establishing limits, possibly illegal as well.

A wildfowl sanctuary or natural-history museum is a good place to start learning wildfowl identification, but there's so much to know that a well-illustrated book is even better in many ways, and every duck hunter should possess one, even if it's the only book he owns. Fortunately, there is a wide choice, ranging from such standard references as Kortright's *The Ducks, Geese and Swans of North America* and standard field guides like Roger Tory Peterson's to the little quickies put out for little or no cost by the Fish and Wildlife Service, Ducks Unlimited, and the large gun

1

RELATIVE SIZE OF—
WILD DUCKS AND GEESE

PINTAIL

MALLARD

BLACK

GADWALL

WIDGEON

SHOVELER

WOOD DUCK

BLUE-WINGED TEAL

CINNAMON TEAL

GREEN-WINGED TEAL

BUFFLEHEAD

RUDDY

RINGNECK

LESSER SCAUP

GREATER SCAUP

GOLDENEYE

REDHEAD

CANVASBACK

HOODED MERGANSER

RED-BREASTED MERGANSER

COMMON MERGANSER

Relative size of Wild Ducks and Geese

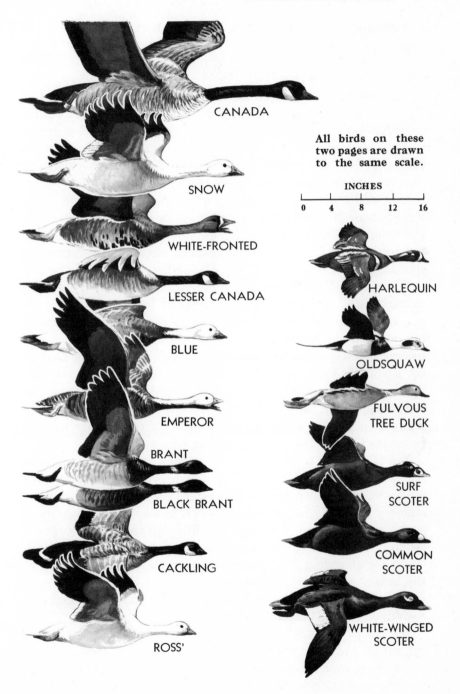

CANADA

SNOW

WHITE-FRONTED

LESSER CANADA

BLUE

EMPEROR

BRANT

BLACK BRANT

CACKLING

ROSS'

**All birds on these
two pages are drawn
to the same scale.**

INCHES

0   4   8   12   16

HARLEQUIN

OLDSQUAW

FULVOUS
TREE DUCK

SURF
SCOTER

COMMON
SCOTER

WHITE-WINGED
SCOTER

and ammunition manufacturers. A selection of the better ones is listed at the end of this chapter, and I urge you to acquire one or more of them at the earliest opportunity if you don't already have one on your shelves.

Such books are basic to the duck hunter's education, but if you can't identify a bird until it's in your hand, it's too late if an error has been made. You must recognize them from afar, and it quickly becomes evident that all those beautiful colors shown on the birds in the picture books are not discernible even within the outer limits of your pitifully short-range shotgun.

It is said that all cats are gray at night. And I know it to be true that all ducks at distance are gray—or black, or white, or in combination. This holds true for aircraft as well as birds, and is the reason the U.S. Air Force teaches aircraft recognition by speedily flashed slides of airplane silhouettes.

The way to learn to recognize flighted ducks is by their flight characteristics, wingbeat, shaded areas of body and wing, plus general appearance. In other words, you recognize an approaching mallard in the same way you recognize your old buddy George coming down the street. You don't have to sum George up as slightly bald, red of face, about six feet in height and two hundred pounds. You automatically say, "Hey, that's good old George." George presented you with many clues to his identity which you spotted instantaneously. You subconsciously noticed his characteristic gait, posture, and overall appearance.

You must learn to identify ducks on the wing in the same manner. You won't be able to name many ducks on your first trip, but no doubt one or two telltale characteristics will be filed in your memory bank. On future outings you'll be more observant about such tip-offs as group formation and flight attitude. Shortly, you'll differentiate at a distance such similar birds as mallards and black ducks by glimpsing the white or silver-appearing underwings of the latter. And once you've seen enough of them, you'll never forget the fast, bunched-together, and low-over-water flight of such diving ducks as cans and bluebills.

We can't disregard color completely, as it is useful in estimating range and as a positive I.D. for closer birds. However, the majority of your recognition will, of necessity, be done at range on gray-appearing birds with only splotches of black and white.

It is your responsibility as a sportsman to know beyond any real doubt what you're shooting at. Split-second identification is often called for, so the safest bet is to start hunting with men of more experience, or to hire a guide. Second best would be to concentrate on identifying only the two or three primary types of ducks you are most likely to encounter on any one trip in a given area. Let the incidental targets pass by until you know them better. If you can identify only mallard, black duck, pintail, and teal, you would still cover the bulk of your bag in puddle-duck shooting. And a man can do quite well at deep-water shooting if he only knows the canvasback, scaup, and redhead.

It's hard to understand how *anyone* could fail to recognize a Canada goose within shotgun range, but its subspecies (cackling, Richardson's, lesser, etc.) can puzzle you for years. A few idiots have mistakenly shot swans for snow geese, which only reinforces my opinion that we should require our hunters to pass a test before receiving their first hunting license, as most European countries do.

You will note that as with most game, male ducks are usually marked much more colorfully and thus are much easier to identify than the females. There are no "drakes only" restrictions

MAJOR WATERFOWL CONCENTRATION AREAS
IN THE UNITED STATES

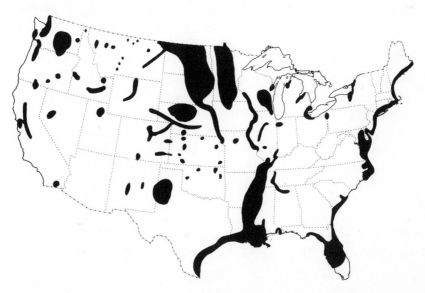

on shooting, but most point systems do much to restrict the shooting of gunners who won't stay away from the girls. However, you'll shoot some hens whether you mean to or not, for all of us have trouble distinguishing hen gadwalls and blacks from the drakes, for example, and many of the females are pretty similar. But try, anyway.

If you are as serious as you should be about identification, you'll set aside time both for book study and field observation of the important members of the duck family. But as a starter, the following may prove helpful.

PUDDLE DUCKS

Most huntable ducks are conveniently divided into two groups. One group is generally called puddle ducks or surface ducks. They are shallow-water or surface-feeding birds, which rarely dive for food. Instead, they dip, sticking their heads under the shallow waters and picking food from the bottom. When alarmed, they seemingly leap straight from the water, although the slow-motion camera has proved they actually *fly* from the surface by powerful downstrokes of their wings. Mostly vegetarians, puddlers are more sought for the table than the diving ducks. Our most important puddle ducks are three varieties of teal, mallard, black duck, pintail, gadwall, wigeon, and wood duck. Of lesser importance to the hunter, but still in the same category, are three others, the spoonbill, ruddy duck, and masked duck.

The mallard

Our top duck! The drake is smarter than his old lady and for this reason is considered a prouder trophy. Many clubs and individuals now pass up hens—a good idea that, if widely followed, can only mean more birds for the future. Then, too, under present point systems two hens puts you out of the duck business for that day, but you can legally take five drakes.

The old greenhead is probably our most widely recognized duck. He feeds in shallow marshes and sloughs, but is also a grazer and cornfielder willing to fly and feed many miles from the nearest body of water. Hunters recognize, but biologists do not, two rather distinct types of mallards. The hunter distinguishes

Our most widely known and easily recognized duck—the drake mallard.

the early or local birds from those that are last to migrate and then fly only as far south as they must go to find open water. This late bird is known among hunters as a "redleg" because of deep orange-red coloring of its legs, compared to the early bird's greenish-yellow color.

The Northern type is a stronger, smarter bird—harder to kill, and cagy when wounded. Because of his full, silk-like feathering he is sometimes called a "puffyhead." Biologists claim he is simply a mature bird that is a late migrant.

The mallard is an easy bird to control through the use of feed, a fact that has often been used to take advantage of him illegally. He decoys readily, and responds to a call better than any other duck. While not above gobbling a few minnows when things are tight, he is among the tastiest of wildfowl, most especially when he can obtain plenty of corn.

The drake's head is an iridescent green set off by a narrow white collar, brick-red breast, and silver-gray belly. The hen is dark brown with tan, U-shaped feather marking. Adult weight averages about 2¾ pounds.

The mallard usually accounts for roughly 35 percent of all ducks bagged in the three western flyways and is rivaled in bag numbers only by the black duck in the Atlantic Flyway.

The black duck

Most gunners will place their money on the black duck (also known as dusky duck or black mallard) as being smartest of all. He looks like a big, very dark mallard hen. Both male and female appear exactly alike at a distance. The black is the most important bird for Eastern duck hunters and also appears in some numbers on the Mississippi Flyway. Its diet varies according to locale. It is considered quite tasty in the East but often passed up by Midwestern gunners because of its habit of eating snails and small late-season shad.

The black is a hard duck to call and decoy, very suspicious of his surroundings. While flying with mallards, blacks will often break formation and leave once the mallards start working decoys. On water, the black usually keeps to his own kind in small groups. Its other habits and flight characteristics are similar to the mallard's.

The pintail (sprig) is surely our most graceful duck in flight. This drake's picture clearly shows his serpentine neck, and the long tail feathers that gave him his name.

An afternoon patrol of pintails. A flight of bull sprig like this is hard to mistake.

The American pintail

The "sprig" is our most graceful-appearing duck in flight. He's rather shy, preferring to remain with his own kind, but will mingle with mallards. He doesn't care for bad weather, preferring to work on sunny afternoons, and most pintails have traveled to warmer climes before the Northern hunter has had much chance at them. Pintails are the number one bird in California, but only some 2 percent of the bag in the Atlantic Flyway.

Perfectly streamlined, the pintail is a splendid flyer and glider. The drake is easily recognized from afar by his long, pointed tail, the large amount of white on his underside, and slender wings. The longer-than-mallard-length neck of both sexes is another important identifying point.

Though the pintail is a puddler and mostly vegetarian, few consider his flesh equal to the mallard as table fare. He works fairly well to mallard decoys and a mallard call, but is usually called by a whistle and worked to decoys of his own type or those carrying a lot of white. Average pintail weight will run 2¼ pounds.

The wood duck

The woody drake is considered our most beautiful duck, as well as fine eating. Since they are not too difficult to bag, they've had a hard time holding their own in numbers. They do not decoy well, but have no hesitation in flying directly over your blocks during the early season. Not particularly hard to hit and not too tenacious of life when crippled, the woody is the only duck I know that dies with its eyes open. It is seldom ever seen in flocks larger than fifty, and the typical wood-duck flight is two to six birds.

As their name implies, wood ducks are tree nesters and quite at home flying through dense timber. Their wingbeat is faster than most puddle ducks. Though they actually have a very square tail, it appears quite long and pointed when viewed horizontally. In numbers bagged, wood ducks rank third in the Atlantic Flyway, second in the Mississippi, eleventh in the Central, and fourth in the Pacific.

The wigeon

Sometimes spelled "widgeon," and known equally well as the "baldpate," the wigeon is a good-eating, sporty duck, mostly taken as a target of opportunity, although there are areas where it is specially hunted (third largest bag in the Pacific Flyway). Though a puddle duck, the wigeon often hangs out with divers, and most books mention its habit of robbing food brought up by the deeper-diving birds.

The drake comes by his nickname from his creamy-white crown. He also wears an elongated green mask which runs over his eyes and back and down his neck. The wigeon's wingbeat is swift for a puddle duck, and it flies in small, compact flocks like divers. However, in their erratic flight wigeon sometimes more closely resemble large teal. Watch for the flashing of the white patches on their forewings.

The gadwall

Though Kortright says of the "gray" duck that "nowhere in its range can it be called abundant," in both Minnesota and Louisiana

Though only an occasional visitor in the Atlantic Flyway, the Gadwall is an important duck in the Central Flyway, and reasonably common in the Mississippi and Pacific.

its numbers account for the second largest bag taken. However, Kortright adds, "It is peculiar in that its distribution is very irregular." So the gadwall is a bird of importance in some places, but only an incidental in others. He is chiefly a vegetarian but, like the black duck, he varies his diet according to locality and the availability of food and thus is ranked much tastier in some areas than in others.

When in small flocks, the gadwall flies swiftly with rapid wing-beats, but he is also often encountered as a loner, flying rather lazily around the edges of the marsh. The drake is a grayish-brown bird with a white speculum and palish brick-red coverts; the grayish-brown hen is sometimes mistaken for the hen red-head. When coming in, gadwalls can be distinguished from mallards by their longer, slimmer wings.

The teal

There are three different teal—blue-winged, green-winged, and cinnamon. The last is of importance only in the West and Southwest. The bluewing is among the first to migrate and so passes through many areas before the start of regular duck hunting. Some states have declared an early, special teal season for this reason. He is a small bird weighing under 1 pound.

Smaller yet is the greenwing, who, though seldom exceeding ¾ pound, is a hardier duck, staying fairly late into Northern seasons. The cinnamon is about the same size. All three teal are great table favorites throughout their range.

Hen teal of all three varieties are best identified by the wing markings that give them their names. Drakes are easier to identify, the blue-winged by the crescent-shaped marking in front of his eyes, the green-winged by a green "mask" not unlike the wigeon's, and the cinnamon by his unmistakably cinnamon breast.

Teal are easy to recognize as a class on the wing because of their small size and very swift, darting, and erratic flight. Flocks will rapidly twist, dodge, and circle in unison, making teal a sporty target. Though hardly slow, because of their small size they appear to fly much faster than they actually do.

Teal are readily identified by their rapid, darting flight and small size, and the blue-winged drake by his crescent-shaped cheek patch.

Not nearly as tough as his expression, the Shoveler is unmistakable even at a distance because of his unique bill.

The shoveler

The poor old "spoonbill" is important only in his numbers killed, mostly by error, though the bill is easy to spot, even from some distance. In full plumage, the green-headed drake remotely resembles the drake mallard, and the spoony hen carries hen-mallard coloring. While the drake is usually pictured in his nuptial plumage, this is a late-winter phase and many Northern hunters have seen him only in his dull, autumn, henlike colors of brown. This has led many to believe they have taken only hen spoonies.

An early migrant, the spoony is usually spotted singly or in pairs, and when shot he appears to fold up from concussion or fright even if missed. Seemingly, one shot pellet will do him in, and the hunter is stuck. (At least, most hunters so believe, for the spoonbill has a bad name among wildfowl gourmets, since about one-third of his diet consists of snails, water beetles, and small minnows. However, the several I have eaten were no worse, or perhaps one degree better, than the more generally eaten blue-bills.) Spoonbills show light-colored wing linings in flight, and that unmistakably large bill.

A courtship flight of shovelers—the lone hen is getting plenty of attention from her suitors!

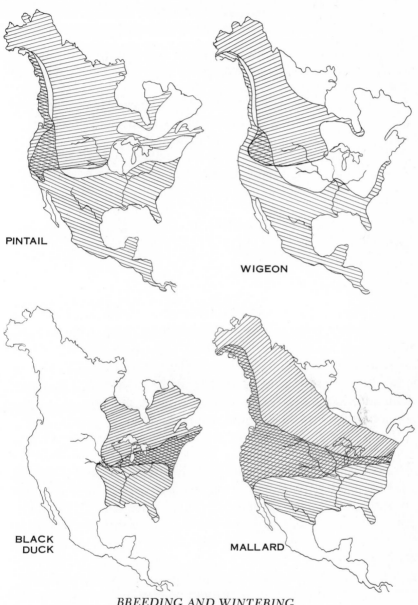

PINTAIL

WIGEON

BLACK DUCK

MALLARD

BREEDING AND WINTERING RANGES OF SOME IMPORTANT DUCKS

Single lines represent northern breeding areas and southern wintering ranges. Cross-hatched areas are both breeding and wintering ranges.

DIVING DUCKS

The diving ducks of greatest importance are the redhead, ring-neck, canvasback, greater and lesser scaup, goldeneye, and buf-flehead. Also in this group are the true sea ducks—old-squaw, harlequin, eider duck, and scoter. These ducks are usually found on large, deep bodies of water such as lakes and coastal bays, though in the interior many are known as "river ducks" because they frequent the larger waterways. They will dive to deep depths for food, and most must taxi along the top of water for a take-off. Except when migrating, most fly very low over the water in tightly packed groups with rapid wingbeats.

Their diet consists largely of marine plant life but with a high· percentage of fish or shellfish which usually ranks them below puddle ducks as table fare.

The canvasback

Once king of the ducks because of his wild-celery diet, he now subsists on whatever is left growing in our polluted lakes and shores. Since diet plays such an important part in the taste of wildfowl, he no longer ranks so highly on the table. On the wing, he is a true sporting bird to hunt—*if* there is a season to hunt him. (The "can" is not doing well in numbers, and many authorities believe he is rapidly losing ground.)

The fastest flyer of all our ducks, the canvasback is not only tough to hit, but hard to capture when crippled. However, he decoys easily, and this has probably led to his downfall. I cut my gunning teeth on cans and recall when you could knock a couple of birds from a flock buzzing your blind, let them swing out, and then call them back again for seconds. Market hunters used to let incoming cans line up, so that two or more could be taken with one shot.

The can is a late migrant who seems to thrive on the foulest weather. He is a large duck, averaging about 3 pounds, and the drake is easily identified by his wedge-shaped dark-red head, and the large amounts of white on the body.

The redhead

I doubt we will ever again have this fine bird in safely hunt-

A drake redhead. Despite a certain superficial similarity to canvasbacks, both size and head shape are sufficiently different so that an observant waterfowler can distinguish between redheads and cans on the wing.

able numbers. While apparently holding his own better than the canvasback, he cannot adapt to the world left him by man, nor can he stand heavy hunting pressure. He often travels with canvasbacks, and less frequently with bluebills. He'll average ½ pound less than the cans and his lighter-colored red and rounded head should make the two species hard to confuse.

The scaup

Both greater and lesser scaup are more widely known as "bluebills" and are also called "broadbills." Greater and lesser scaup are difficult to distinguish from each other, but for the hunter it is a matter of little importance. Their marine diet does not make them a particularly good eating duck. In years past they existed in great numbers and I've seen rafts of bluebills that stretched for over a mile. Though they reached a dangerously low population after World War II, they seem to have increased nicely in the last few years.

Scaup are hard, fast-flying ducks that readily respond to calling and decoys. The drakes are distinguished at a distance by their white belly and sides contrasting with their black-appearing breast and head. The lesser scaup averages about 1¾ pounds with the greater running only ¼ pound more.

Ring-necked duck

Even the most experienced hunter has difficulty distinguishing the "blackjack" from bluebills at a distance, though they usually fly in somewhat smaller groups and a wider formation. They are also a better eating duck than bluebills, since about four-fifths of their food is aquatic vegetation. Ringnecks decoy readily, and once so inclined, come busting straight into the blocks. Seldom found in great numbers, they account for only about 5 percent of the bag in all four flyways. They are sometimes called ringbills because of the small white band across the bill, and this is

Four scaup drakes (bluebills).

actually a much easier distinguishing mark than the pale, indistinct ring around the neck. Like the scaups, ringnecks have short tails and noticeably use their feet as balancing airfoils when coming in to land.

The goldeneye

The "whistler" comes in two varieties, the common or American goldeneye, and Barrow's goldeneye. The latter is a western bird which has a crescent-shaped white face patch instead of a round one. A flock of goldeneye once heard will never be forgotten; their wings make a loud whistling in flight. In some areas they are known as an "ice duck," for they seemingly enjoy arctic conditions. They usually migrate in small flocks at high altitude. Wary birds, they do not readily decoy and are generally taken through pass shooting. They are strictly third-rate table fare, though otherwise a pretty and fascinating little duck. The common goldeneye weighs about 2 pounds and the larger Barrow's about 2¾.

The bufflehead

The "butterball" has a similar flight and behavior pattern to the goldeneye, and there is little to distinguish between the two except for the bufflehead drake's large white face patch behind his eye, and the smaller white face patch of the hen. Butterballs do, however, fly quite low above the water, which is some help in separating them from the goldeneye. They are also more numerous throughout their range.

OTHER DUCKS

Unimportant to the hunter but necessary for him to recognize (if only to avoid) are the mergansers or fish ducks. There are three of them—common, red-breasted, and hooded. They feed on small fish and crustaceans and taste terrible, and for this reason total less than 1 percent of the take in all flyways.

Sea ducks, such as the scoters, are known primarily to coastal hunters with only a few "accidentals" sifting through interior flyways. The oldsquaw, while found in some numbers on the Great

Morning flight of lesser snow and blue geese. While the blue is still spoken of separately, and was once considered a distinct species, it is actually only a color phase of the lesser snow goose.

Lakes, is also essentially a sea duck. The eider, a Far Northern duck, accounts for less than 1 percent of our bag.

There are two tree ducks traveling a small area of the Southwest, and a few "area" ducks, but most hunters will never be called upon to know them.

THE GEESE

Ninety percent of our hunters will be concerned with identification of only four geese. The widely recognized Canadas and their subspecies the lesser Canadas look alike except for size. The white-fronted goose, or "specklebelly," is limited mostly to the Central and Pacific flyways. Snow geese are divided into "greater," an Eastern Seaboard flock, and "lesser," which is common to the other three flyways. While still usually defined separately and once thought a different species, the blue goose is now known to be but a color phase of the lesser snow goose. Having never hunted brant, I am qualified only to quote Kortright: "The black brant is a strictly maritime species of the Pacific Coast—it closely resembles the American brant of the Atlantic Coast."

THE COOT

The American coot, sometimes called "water chicken," is much more widely known as the "mudhen." They are widely distributed, little hunted, and vastly underrated on the table. Coot inhabit salt bays, marshes, ponds, and rivers in great number during the duck season. The mudhen is a little, gray-black bird with a bone-white beak. He doesn't fly high and he's not very speedy, as waterfowl go. He is also rather trusting, since he is not considered a bragging bird among those who take their ducking

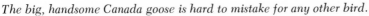

The big, handsome Canada goose is hard to mistake for any other bird.

seriously and doesn't have to duck much lead. His lobed toes
make him a great swimmer but prevent him from leaping from
the water, so he needs a lot of runway to taxi along and gain
flying speed. Pushing a boat through the marsh to jump coot can
prove most productive and offer the new shooter many chances
for shots at all angles. Since the bird will often be shot at only a
foot or so above the water, the splash made by the shot pattern
will be very helpful in giving the shooter a better understanding
of the amount of lead required. This, plus his ample numbers,
makes the coot a fine bird for the novice waterfowler to cut his
teeth on.

SUGGESTED IDENTIFICATION MANUALS

HINES, BOB. *Ducks at a Distance.* Washington: Bureau of Sports
Fisheries & Wildlife, 1961. (For sale by the Superintendent

*Despite a large wing-span, the American coot must taxi quite a ways on
its odd, lobed toes before it can take off.*

of Documents, U.S. Government Printing Office.) The color is poor, but there is an excellent silhouette chart of comparative sizes.

KORTRIGHT, F. H. *The Ducks, Geese and Swans of North America.* Harrisburg, Pa.: Stackpole, 1967. The standard work.

PETERSON, ROGER TORY. *A Field Guide to the Birds,* Boston: Houghton-Mifflin, 1947.

RUTHVEN, J. A., and ZIMMERMAN, WM. *Top Flight Speed Index to Waterfowl of North America.* Milwaukee: Moebius Press, 1965.

SPRUNT, A., IV, and ZIM, H.S. *Gamebirds.* New York: Golden Press, 1961.

WYLIE, S. R. and FURLONG, S.S. *Key to North American Waterfowl.* Wynnewood, Pa.: Livingston Publishing Co., 1972. One of the shortest, but one of the most practical to take into the blind—it is printed on waterproof paper!

2.
The
Well-Dressed
Duck Hunter

Assuming that you now know what a duck looks like, we can turn to what a duck hunter looks like, which is to say, what he wears. In this respect if no other, today's wildfowler has it all over the old-timers, who did their shooting when the state of the art of thermal clothing was somewhat less well advanced than it is today. For many decades it was easy enough to describe what duck hunters looked like in one word, and that word was "cold."

When I was a kid in the mid-1930s, duck seasons ran late into winter, and we all damn near froze. When you hunted ducks, your hands and feet were always cold and the fact was accepted as a matter of course. Involuntary shivering stopped only when birds were working your decoys. We wore stiff canvas coats, made stiffer by a home waterproofing of gasoline and paraffin. Our equally stiff black rubber boots were insulated with whatever loose duck down we could stuff down their sides.

Working outward from the skin, our clothing started with a union suit (replete with trapdoor) and proceeded with a flannel shirt, a heavy, home-knit sweater, and a horsehide vest, all of which did little to contain body heat.

But that was long ago. It's a wonder we survived (though we

24

did, and thought it great sport). In any case, today's hunter need never know such discomfort. Yet many do, simply because they still cling to old ideas or don't know any better. Writers still preach the layered principle of clothing even though we have insulated one-piece garments that are lighter in weight and far warmer than any number of layers you could wear and still swing a gun.

I've often pitied those whose geographic location restricts them to mild-weather hunting. To me, the battle against the elements is almost as satisfying as the hunt itself. However, more deserving of pity are probably those poor souls who chase ducks in foul weather without proper equipment. Warm, comfortable clothing is often the only difference between a marvelous day and a completely miserable one.

WHAT SIZE?

I've been in the outdoor clothing and equipment business for many years and at all levels—retail, wholesale, and design. I honestly believe that 80 percent of our hunters, experienced or not, have little idea of what clothing to buy, or the size they need. The question of size is perhaps the most perplexing, yet most neglected, problem in choosing outdoor clothing.

Good hunting duds last a long time, with or without care. A first-class hunting coat by a reputable manufacturer can be expected to stand up and serve well for a minimum of five years, and often double that. By the time most of us acquire enough taste, knowledge, and cash to buy a really good coat, we are approaching middle age and ought to consider what poundage the good life may add to us within the next decade. But even aside from this, if error in size is to be made, it is best to err on the large side for other reasons. The clothing will be worn during strenuous activity when freedom of movement is most desirable. It may also be worn over other garments, necessitating perhaps a full size, or even two full sizes, larger than your street clothes. For instance, when buying trousers, remember that a heavy wool shirt and insulated underwear will require at least one waist size larger than your regular suit pants.

The same goes for boots. I recommend that you always buy

your hunting boots, whether leather or rubber, at least a half-size longer and one width wider than you normally wear. Those taking a 10-D street shoe will most certainly need at least a 10½-E boot. This is not only because of the heavier socks you will wear but also because your feet tend to expand during long periods of walking or standing. Most importantly, *a tight boot is a cold boot* no matter what it is stuffed with. Rubber boots should be bought even larger. Whether insulated or not, you will probably wear boot liners or a couple pairs of socks. Since rubber retains foot moisture, socks and liners often become sodden and if pressed tightly around the foot, invariably lead to cold toes.

Even the very best of underwear tends to shrink in washing, so buy it large, too. It will be warmer and give less feeling of confinement.

Probably the only item of clothing that should be a snug fit is your shooting gloves, and these must provide the same sense of security in gun handling to which we are accustomed bare-handed.

Now that the preliminaries are out of the way, let's take clothing categorically.

FOOTGEAR

Though boots for duck hunting always means rubber, their height depends upon conditions. Few of us can get by with less than hip boots (which might better be called "crotch" boots), while for some conditions, full waders are even better. Regardless of their length, rubber boots should be purchased from a busy store. The box in which they come should have a clean, new appearance because whether in use or not, rubber oxidizes and deteriorates with age. A pair of boots that has spent a couple of years on the dealer's shelf may give less service than if they had been worn for the same period. Few of us "wear out" hip boots. Rather, the rubber loses its strength and flexibility—cracks, rots, or otherwise falls apart.

So it is not mere patriotism that recommends buying American-made rubber boots. I know of no American firm using reclaimed rubber, which is the chief ingredient of many low-priced, imported products. In addition, good American-made rubber contains a formula of several special ingredients that effectively prolong its useful life.

Good boots deserve good care, not so much when you are wearing them as when you aren't. A duck hunter's boots are often used only one month out of the year and put in storage the rest of the time. How they are stored has a lot to do with how much service they'll give.

First of all, hip boots and waders should never be put away folded. Draw them out to full length. Wire boot hangers are available, or you can make your own by bending old clothes hangers. Hang them by the *foot*, preferably in a cool, dark, and dry area. Before storing, wash with detergent and water to rid them of grease, gasoline, and mud that can quickly deteriorate the rubber.

Insulated boots

No matter how temperate the weather in which you hunt, water is always cold, and I can see little reason for any wildfowler

Thanks to modern insulated boots and waders, today's hunter can stand icy water all day.

buying uninsulated boots. The type of insulation varies some-what with the manufacturer, but most good-quality insulation is of soft-plastic foam, and the best is known as unicell. This simply means each air cell is sealed and separate.

The open-cell type of insulation is nearly as warm, but since the cells interconnect, a boot puncture (as from an exposed nail in the blind) will allow water to seep through the insulation, and leave you little chance of ever being able to completely dry the boot.

There are a few models of over-the-shoe boots. These are uninsulated and depend on your socks and shoes to contain warmth. They are sometimes chosen for use in deep mud as the shoe helps relieve pressure on the foot.

Hip boots

Whenever their height is adequate, hip boots are more com-fortable than waders. They can be made even more so by the use of suspenders or a boot harness which places the weight on the shoulders rather than tugging down your pants, as occurs when regular belt loops are worn. Other advantages of hip boots over waders are that they are easier to put on and take off, and facilitate the numerous calls of nature that plague most hunters. They also dispel foot moisture better than longer types of gear. Incidentally, when they've finally had it, don't just toss them away. Mend the foot with a cold tire patch and cut off the tops below the knee. You now have a convenient slip-on boot for boat use.

Waders

In deeper water waders become a necessity. Waist waders are not the answer. They do a good job of keeping your behind dry on a wet boat seat, but offer only about 10 inches more protection than hip boots. So when I speak of waders, I mean chest height. Sure, they are cumbersome, hard to walk in, and hot, and they confine body moisture. But they are often the only answer when working on soft, muddy bottoms or in murky water with entangle-ments. They prevent many an accidental bath and allow you to shoot from places otherwise inaccessible. The trout fisherman's trick of wearing an oversized belt around his waist, outside the waders, is an essential precaution, limiting the volume of water you'll take on board if you happen to stumble.

Few people realize how American-brand waders are proportioned. Most are available in short, regular, and long, which involves not only total height but also the length of crotch. Any duck hunter of average height or taller will probably find the longs better for his use. On the average guy they may look like holy hell, bagging at the crotch and showing deep folds throughout their length. However, accordion pleats are precisely what is needed for kneeling and climbing in and out of boat and blind. If you buy a pair of waders that are too short, something will rip somewhere in due time.

Nylon-top waders are lighter and more flexible, though a bit more costly. I doubt that they last any longer than all-rubber models, but I think they're worth the extra cost in comfort.

Drying boots

When worn daily, all boots become wet inside from foot moisture. A simple solution is to stuff them at night with loosely wadded newspapers, which will absorb much of the wetness. Rubber boots should never be subjected to the direct heat of a fire, nor should a burning light bulb, even of low wattage, be put in them. However, there are electric boot dryers on the market (such as the Ronning, made in Norway) which are satisfactory. These are thermostatically controlled to a low, steady heat not injurious to the rubber. Another fast, safe dryer, should one be available, is a canister-type vacuum cleaner with the hose on "blower." The use of powder is not recommended—it only cakes after use. The best solution for anyone wearing boots daily is to have two pairs and alternate them. And if you can't do anything else, at least turn the legs inside out overnight.

Boot liners

Boot liners were in more general use before the advent of insulated boots, but they still have their place and are preferred by many hunters. The oldest types are sheepskin and felt. The genuine fleece-in sheepskin has become difficult to find in many sections of the country. They not only make pretty fair boot liners but excellent camp slippers. They come up about ankle height

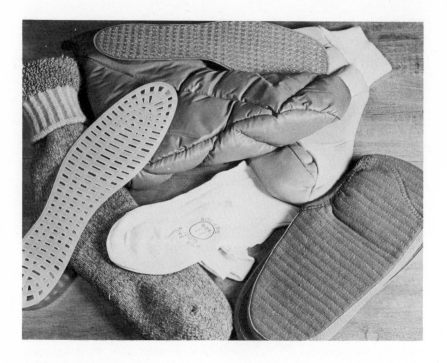

Part of the large choice of boot socks, liners and insoles available to the modern wildfowler (clockwise from top): Vent-O-Sole, foam-filled sock, German Bama liner, raw silk undersock, Dutch Skenke insole, thermal-knit sock, goose down liner.

and the fleece insulates and cushions your feet. Some are now being made with a synthetic fleece, which probably wears well and is just as warm. The drawback to either type is they retain foot moisture and require a lot of room in the boot.

Recently there's been a return to popularity of the old pressed-felt liner. These came back as part of an oversized short boot that is quite warm and useful for ice fishing, deer stands, or, in some cases, the duck blind, though heavy and awkward for walking any great distance. However, the felt liners may be bought separately and work fine in insulated hip boots and waders. Make sure your boots are large enough to accept them.

In my experience, goosedown booties don't work very well. The boot compresses the down and leaves little insulative loft.

There is a modern product, however, that's the best liner I've found for rubber footwear of any kind. It is German-made and sells under various trade names such as Bama and Sokket. It is designed to prevent foot moisture in both insulated and regular rubber boots. Its inner lining of synthetic hair condenses perspiration and carries it by capillary action to the fleecy cotton outerlining where it is absorbed. When worn with light or medium socks these liners will keep your feet dry all day, and *dry feet are warm feet.*

Another modern form of liner is the insulated-foam boot sock. These are usually made three-layered—a soft cotton or nylon fleece inside, a thin layer of foam insulating material, and a nylon outer covering. They, too, are warm in the boot, and are excellent for wearing to bed in a cold cabin.

Innersoles

When it's not too cold, some hunters prefer an innersole. Its main purpose is to keep the foot off the cold bottom of the boot, but some are also designed to absorb foot moisture; and they can, of course, be easily removed for drying. Perhaps the oldest

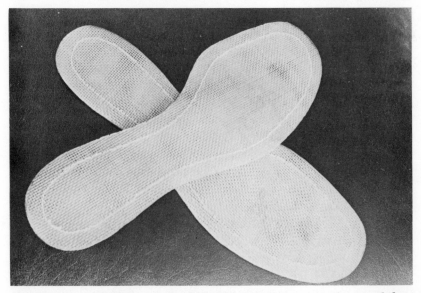

Plastic-mesh insoles place a layer of insulating air between your foot and the cold bottom of the boot.

designs are cork and pressed felt. Both do an adequate job and are still available in northern parts of the country.

There are also newer materials, used in insoles designed with a different idea in mind. Some of these are made from a semi-soft plastic perforated with air holes, allowing air to be circulated under the foot with each step. This theory has been proved successful by the Canadian Army, which issues a screen-type insole that, to my knowledge, is not available commercially. However, the average man can make the same thing for himself. Simply purchase a section of nylon or plastic window screen, trace the outline of your foot, and cut four or more layers to be stacked one atop another. They can be used as cut, or if you wish a neater job, bind or melt the edges, sanding off any sharp surplus. This makes a most efficient insole for keeping the feet warm and socks dry.

Socks

Cotton socks are about the worst possible choice for use in rubber footgear. About all they do is soak up moisture, leaving your feet clammy all day. Wool is better, feeling warm even when damp. But some of the new synthetic materials or synthetic-wool blends are even better still. Socks containing Olefin and Rhovyl actually wick moisture away from the feet. Another good choice is the Austrian-type thermal sock now made here. This is an inside terry-knit fabric with thousands of overlapping little loops to pad your feet and give good insulation.

In practice, socks aren't so important with good insulated rubber boots, and the traditional wearing of two or more pairs of socks is seldom to be recommended in view of the new and better insulating materials now used. One traditional fabric, seemingly overlooked until the skiers rediscovered it, is raw silk. A silk innersock worn under your regular stockings adds warmth with little bulk and is a good blister preventive. These are now standard Navy issue for arctic and antarctic wear, and anyone troubled with excess foot perspiration should at least give them a try. Those who have this problem are also well advised to sprinkle their bare feet liberally with bromidrosis powder, available at any drugstore.

UNDERWEAR

The old one-piece wool or cotton trapdoor-model longjohns were at one time most popular. Today, we find the two-piece design superior, allowing you to add or subtract top or bottom as needed.

Of these, there are two distinct types. One is the quilted and insulated, which is filled, depending upon price, with everything from goosedown to cotton batting. Most are very warm—many, much too warm. While goosedown is our very best insulating material for outer garments, it is not particularly satisfactory in underwear. This is because down depends upon loft for its insulating effect, and being easily compressed, loses a great deal of its value when worn under other clothing.

A less resilient insulation is called for. Perhaps the best is Dacron 88, although much the same type of synthetic material goes under other well-known brand names. The biggest problem with quilted-type underwear is the bulk on which it depends for warmth. Some find it restricts body movement and makes their regular outer clothing uncomfortably tight. For this reason I prefer quilted underwear, insulated with the soft-plastic foam known as Curon or Scott-Foam. This seems to offer all the warmth of the "stuffed" variety but without bulk. Regardless of the filling, unless you're hunting the Arctic, insulated underwear offers more warmth than necessary. I seldom use the pants, and notice most underwear jackets being worn over the shirt for quick removal, rather than next to the skin where they are more efficient.

Most of us get by quite nicely with a more conventional form of underwear such as the excellent two-layer Duofold. This comes in many models and choices of fabrics. Most commonly it combines a layer of cotton next to the skin with an outer layer of wool, but even a cashmere blend is available for the luxury lover.

Another new development, and an excellent one, is a French synthetic called Rhovyl. It was developed for insulation in rubber skin-diving suits and actually wicks away body moisture from the inner to outer layer where it is more easily expelled. It is unbelievably warm and comfortable for its very light weight. Another is a type of waffle weave used by many manufacturers and it, too, has proved itself over the years.

Probably the most controversial undergarment is the Scandinavian "fishnet," or string, underwear. This is usually made of cotton netting with fairly large holes, the principle being to trap insulating air between the body and the outer garments. It's particularly admired by those who must be both in and out of doors, because of its light weight and feeling of freedom. I can personally recommend the tops, or shirts, but have found the pants uncomfortable on the knees when kneeling in a blind.

SHIRTS

With proper sleeve length, enough shoulder room, and a neutral color, almost any shirt will do the duck hunter. Nonetheless, there are pitfalls. While wool is warm, comfortable, and long-lasting, it must have a neck lining of cotton, rayon, or nylon. Duck hunting requires constant watching and scanning of the skies, which means considerable head movement, and plain wool next to the neck will scratch, redden, and quickly tenderize the skin. Should you have to go several days' running with the same shirt, wool against the skin can become almost unbearable.

Because of this, my personal shirt preference has always been the double-faced cotton variously known as doeskin, moleskin, or chamois cloth. It is warm, windproof, and very comfortable, becoming softer with each washing. It doesn't itch or chafe the skin in any way. It is made in several colors, but under average fall conditions the duck hunter will do well to stay with the natural chamois tan. There are only two or three mills in the country that manufacture this fabric. It is made in two weights, the heaviest of which is preferable in any type of weather. Make sure you buy a long-tailed model, rather than square-tail, as nothing is quite so uncomfortable as a short-tailed shirt that keeps coming out of your pants and exposing skin areas.

Whatever shirt you wear should have button-flap pockets to prevent losing overboard whatever they contain. Buttons have a way of coming off, and fabric buttonholes enlarge. Some of the fine patented snap systems seem the best answer but are often hard to find on a shirt of your choice. Velcro tape closures are good but also hard to find. A safety pin is better than leaving a loose flap.

Almost any heavy shirt, whether wool or chamois cloth, can be improved by a double cape shoulder, and while there are two excellent wool models made by Woolrich a double cape is practically impossible to find in chamois cloth.

PANTS

I'm not exactly sure what the best duck-hunting trousers would be, but with deep apologies to my Texas friends, I'll sure say that Western-style blue jeans are the worst. They are cold, tight-crotched, and leg-binding. Of course, I hardly expect that anything I say here will dethrone them from their number one position with the Western hunter.

However, I can't endorse the standard Eastern product, either. My personal choice in duck pants would be a softer material than the common stiff duck or khaki. They would have a double seat, preferably with a layer of rubber sandwiched between. Pockets would be sewn, bar-tacked, and riveted at point of stress. A large front zipper of nylon or Delrin that can be put back on track is a must. Deep sailcloth pockets with double bottoms would help. The pants would have both suspender buttons and wide belt loops. All seams would be at least double-stitched. I would buy them cuffless, cut to ankle height and in one waist size larger to accommodate underwear and a heavy shirt. Hip pockets would have button or snap flaps and be placed high enough on the hips to accommodate wallet, handkerchief, and what-have-you without being sat on. I would like identical pants in a medium-weight blend of 80 percent wool/20 percent nylon for cold-weather use, and a medium-weight blend of 65 percent cotton/35 percent Dacron for early-season use.

That is what I would like, but as of this writing no manufacturer has seen fit to produce such a design.

COATS

For early season in the South, or some of our Western states, any lightweight canvas field coat is adequate. Often these areas still have some green vegetation and many hunters find lightweight camouflage jackets in greenish hues ideal. Some patterns are in more "fallish" colors of tans and browns.

For most of us hunting colder areas, lightweight jackets will not do. For real cold-weather hunting, coats insulated with goose-down are hard to beat. Down's comfort range is far greater than that afforded by any other type of insulation. Down has the happy faculty of wisping away body moisture so that when you become overheated by slogging through the mud from shore to blind, or strenuous rowing, you do not become sweat-soaked and sit out the rest of the day risking a cold or pneumonia.

Despite its expense, good goosedown insulation should certainly receive primary consideration from anyone who expects to hunt very often under severe weather conditions. The effectiveness of down, as with any other insulation, depends on trapping still air. Goosedown of good grade has a higher loft, or

A good duck or goose down vest will let you use your lightweight hunting coat comfortably in colder weather, too.

springiness, than most duckdown and, therefore, will give more warmth for less weight. However, it is a minor difference in a jacket whether it is stuffed with goosedown or duckdown, and often quite a saving can be made by choosing the latter.

I cannot recommend the many insulated one-piece suits or jumpers for duck hunting. They are very warm but do not allow enough ventilation of the body to keep you dry if any strenuous activity is involved.

For years we've been told that for warmth we should use layered clothing, and this is not a bad idea, although well-insulated garments make it unnecessary. For those hunting in both warm and severely cold weather, however, a down vest under a medium-weight coat is often a very good compromise. And you can always shed the vest as the day warms up.

Whatever type of jacket you choose, it should have certain features, the principal one being an attached or detachable hood or parka. No matter how warm the coat, you are always warmer wearing a parka hood. It prevents drafts and snow down the neck, keeps the ears from freezing, and if cut sufficiently back from the sides of the face, will not interfere with gun pointing.

A rear game pocket is not necessary, but it is often handy—to carry raingear, lunch, Thermos, and the other niceties of a duck hunter's life. It's optional and a personal choice. However, every hunting coat needs good body pockets and preferably slash handwarmer pockets. The cargo pockets should be of the bellows type for carrying gloves and shells. They should be bar-tacked and riveted at points of stress, and double-lined for long wear. The elastic web shell holders are handy for isolating special shells such as cripple and goose loads.

The coat should fasten with an oversized zipper which must be covered with a button or snap wind-tab. A zippered coat without wind-tab is an evil thing—the slightest breeze going through the zipper teeth can nullify the effectiveness of any type of insulation.

Ideal coat length is fingertip unless you normally wear waders, in which case a short waist jacket will probably be more comfortable. Avoid a fur collar. No matter how good it feels snugged up against your neck in the store, it won't feel that way when it's wet from rain or snow. A knit collar is handy to shoot in, as,

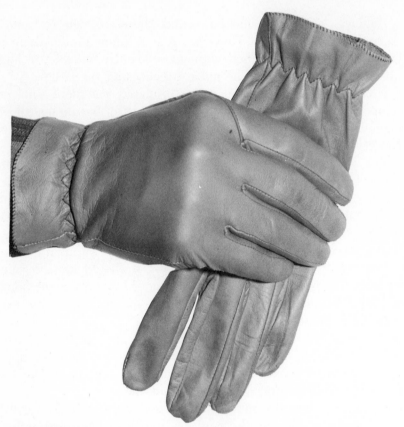

Some insulated gloves are too cumbersome to permit proper feel of the trigger. These thin capeskin gloves have an inner liner of Curon foam; they are warm but still soft and flexible.

when worn open, there is nothing to get between the gun and the shoulder. But a knit collar is very likely to chafe the neck. Much better is a short, padded collar of the same material as the coat or of wide-wale corduroy. Cuffs with outside knit wristlets also become wet, but a straight or suitcoat-type cuff with an inner knit wristlet stops the breeze from going up your sleeve.

Any insulated coat should have an inside drawstring to snug it around the waist. This drawstring is not tied and untied each time you wear the coat—rather, it is looped and tied on each side to fit and left that way so the jacket will be the same each time you wear it.

A good outer fabric is a cotton/nylon or Dacron blend in a high-count poplin. These fabrics are usually treated with some form of waterproofing, which simply means that you'll get wet when it rains. But again, I wouldn't take a completely waterproof jacket under any circumstances. It would not allow body moisture to escape, and would be like wearing a Thermos bottle. I'd rather use the separate foul-weather gear that is discussed later on.

You have a wide choice in colors. A suitable shade against any background for duck hunting is dead grass and the brown forms of camouflage. My personal choice is a German field gray (riverbottom-mud gray, if you wish), but this shade is difficult to find. Check out Canadian and English-made coats of a superb fabric called Falcon or Grenfell cloth. This is a very-high-count cotton poplin with basic background color of dead grass very sparsely interwoven with fibers of iridescent green and brown. It's a long-wearing, windproof, and beautiful-appearing cloth that blends well with almost any vegetation anywhere.

Some hunters apply their own camouflage to a taupe or dead-grass-colored fabric by applying streaks of various dyestuffs. This usually calls for some experimentation as no two fabrics take dye in the same way.

The so-called "action-back" garments give the most freedom in shooting, but this design is not always available on an otherwise desirable coat. Just keep in mind raglan shoulders will always allow more freedom than an inset sleeve.

To prolong the life of a good hunting coat, it is a simple matter for a smart wife to bind the cuffs and pocket edges with soft leather. If you happen to have married the other kind, you can usually be accommodated by any tailor or even an automobile-upholstery shop.

GLOVES

A duck hunter's gloves must be thick enough to keep the hands warm, yet thin enough to give "feel." Thick, heavy gloves for gun handling are an abomination. Yet the very thin skin-tight leather gloves preferred by clay target shooters are not warm enough for cold-weather use. So some smart cookie used this same extra thin split leather, but lined it with a thin insulating foam and then added an innerliner of silk (which adds warmth with little bulk to any glove). The combination makes the best of all insulated shooting gloves. Whatever warmth your hands produce, this glove will hold. The only people I've found who are not satisfied with them are those with poor circulation, whose hands produce little heat.

These gloves, as with most good things in life, are relatively expensive. They also get wet, and while it doesn't hurt the glove, they do lose their warmth. Of course, the skin areas of the hand must breathe, too, and a waterproof glove is no good for continuous use.

What are the alternatives? I've tried to use heavy mittens with a palm-cut flap which allows you to instantly stick out your trigger-pulling finger, but they give me a deep feeling of insecurity for holding on to the gun.

There is a patented wool glove with leather trigger finger that has proved quite satisfactory. There are good wool gloves as well as a wool and raccoon-hair mixture with soft leather palms that are warm. There are some soft-leather, fleece-lined gloves that are not too thick for trigger use (though they too get wet, a condition we must accept as a fact of duck hunting). My own preference, after many years of experimenting, is to carry several pairs of the very inexpensive brown cotton jersey work gloves that are sold through most any hardware or grocery store. They are warm and flexible, and as one pair becomes wet you simply replace it with a dry pair.

The only time you need a pair of waterproof gloves is for picking up the decoys, but you sure need them then. They can be rubber, vinyl, or any other noncold-cracking plastic. Some are lined with "flock" for greater warmth and all are worth their weight in gold at pick-up time. My favorite is the long gauntlet type sold for industrial use in working around acids. They are usually made of neoprene and seemingly last forever. Buy the thinner weight and you will also have an ideal glove for gutting out big game in cold weather. Always buy "pick-up" gloves in size extra-large regardless of your hand size. It makes them easy to put on and take off, and they will fit over your regular gloves.

I haven't found electrically heated gloves or mittens satisfactory in any way. Those using two C-cell batteries are exhausted in a couple of hours. Consequently, anyone hunting a twelve-hour day must carry a dozen heavy and expensive batteries. But for those afflicted with arthritis of the fingers, they may be worth the trouble and money.

HEADGEAR

You can run around town bareheaded, but don't try it for cold-weather hunting. The percentage of total body-heat loss attributable to the top of the head has been estimated at 20 to 50, depending on whose figures you read. Few will deny that keeping warm in severe weather calls for some type of headgear, but the exact type is a sticky subject. Headgear is a highly personal choice for most of us, and hats are often worn more for their personality than functional use. Geographic location enters strongly into the choice, doesn't it, Tex?

As a personal choice, I wear a wool-knit tanker cap or wool-knit Navy watchcap. Both are soft, comfortable, and unlikely to blow off in the strongest wind. They also fit well under a parka hood. But then so do other types that are more wind- and rainproof. Down-filled caps are very warm (usually too warm) and always bulky. The wide-brimmed hats protect from rain, but catch wind and branches.

So long as it is a neutral color, stays on the head, and is comfortable, choose whatever hat or cap suits your fancy.

RAINGEAR

Raingear comes in many shapes and sizes, but it all boils down to only two types—good and bad. The good is a most essential item; the bad is not only worthless, but possibly dangerous to your health.

The last decade has seen our market flooded with imported rainwear at fantastically low prices. Some of it is quite adequate for the man dodging raindrops from street curb to office door, but very little of this cheap, easily torn plastic or shoddy rubber can be considered seriously by the hunter. For when it comes to raingear, "water-repellent" is not enough. Good foul-weather gear must be absolutely waterproof, and remain so with certainty.

If rubber is used, it should be a virgin grade, either natural

The camouflaged, waterproof duck parka comes in shades of tan and brown that are much better suited to late season foliage than the usual, predominantly green patterns.

or synthetic. It must resist cracking with cold, and tackiness with heat. The better grades have a rubber layer sandwiched between two layers of fiber material. The cheaper makes are usually inside- or outside-coated, exposing the rubber surfaces to contact with each other. This means rubber can stick to rubber and pull it from the bonding material.

Properly made rubber garments are certainly not obsolete, but there have been great improvements in synthetic coatings now used on nylon. They make compact gear of light weight which seems to retain its waterproofing qualities indefinitely.

There is no all-purpose raingear, for the requirements of the camper or warm-weather fisherman differ widely from those of

Some hunters prefer hard cases, but I find a soft shell bag with shoulder strap handiest for camera, lunch, raingear, etc.

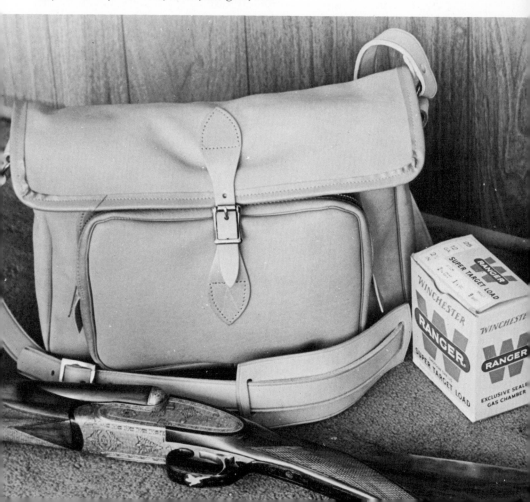

the duck hunter. Even so, their raingear shares a bad habit in common. All waterproof garments collect body moisture, and if you are active enough to work up a good sweat, these droplets of moisture condense until it looks as if your gear has sprung a leak.

No one has found a satisfactory method of eliminating this fault. Good rainsuits are usually ventilated across the back under a double cape shoulder. Some have eyelets under the armpits, and others have devised porous materials supposedly waterproof, yet breathable. But none has proved itself to general satisfaction. Condensation of body moisture is a fact we should accept, at least for the moment, and not blame our rain garments for doing a poor job.

When wearing hip boots or waders, only a short-length rain parka is needed. Converse Hodgman and Fredericks Rubber Co. both have made the same pattern of duck-hunting parka for many years. Either brand is completely satisfactory for its purpose. Both are made in a dead-grass color or a brown camouflage pattern. They hold up in brush and brambles and take some determination to rip. They are cut low enough under the armpits for fit and freedom over heavy jackets. But again, the prospective buyer must keep in mind the type of clothing he intends to be wearing under the rain garment and buy a large enough size to ensure this fit and freedom.

Both of the above-named American firms also make a three-quarter-length parka in the same colors and patterns. They are short, though still rather lengthy for wading. Both brands cost roughly three times the price of cheaper, imported merchandise that looks very much the same. In practice, though, the more costly garments will prove less expensive in the long run and give far better foul-weather protection.

3.
The
Duck Gun

M ost everyone agrees a shotgun is the best weapon to use on ducks, but from that point on, there is little agreement on anything pertaining to the matter. A gun is a highly personal object, reflecting individual tastes and preferences as well as the conditions under which the individual shoots.

Of course, there are minimum standards among those calling themselves sportsmen, as well as maximums that we must observe to remain on the right side of the law. Our present federal laws forbid shooting anything larger than the 10-gauge, but allow use of the .410, which is the smallest true scattergun we've got. This is too bad, in a way, because for those who can handle it, the 8-gauge was, and would be still, a great duck gun, while the .410 should be unthinkable for wildfowling. A dead duck is only so dead, but a cripple is a cripple whether winged with the illegal 8-gauge or the legal .410. This is not to say that I'm advocating restoring the 8-gauge or pushing for abolition of the sub-small-bore. Rather, it is to say the average hunter will find it more sensible to restrict his choice to the gauges from 20 to 12.

So what is the ideal duck gun? It's not that simple. There are a lot of factors to consider, and I'd suggest that we begin with the matter of gauge, as there should be less argument here than on any other point. And let's start off by looking at the standard 12.

THE 12-GAUGE

The 12-gauge is the far-ahead favorite of the American duck hunter. It is a ballistically efficient gauge, able to perform well with many different shot sizes and shell loadings. It is large enough to contain an adequate number of pellets for a dead-certain kill at reasonable ranges. Its bore size is large enough to maintain a short shot string of these pellets, and it is now loaded to the maximum velocity at which you can still obtain good pattern percentages.

The average 12-gauge duck gun will weigh 8 pounds or less—light enough for those of average strength to handle quickly and

Duck guns come in every type of action. Ordinarily they have longer barrels, tighter chokes and weigh more than field guns. Three-shot pump or auto repeaters are more popular than doubles, but I've always liked over-and- unders like these. The gun with the extra sets of barrels is a Winchester, and the hunter is holding a Richland.

easily, yet heavy enough to restrict recoil to tolerable limits. Its shells are offered in far more different loadings than any other gauge, and are readily available anywhere shotgun shells are sold. The 12 is made in every type of action and in more models than any other gauge.

Though a few die-hards swear by it, I'd have to eliminate the 16-gauge from consideration. Sure, it's got a shorter shot string than the 20 if both are loaded with the same amount of shot, and sure, it handles an ounce of shot very nicely indeed. But as a practical matter, it's something of a dead issue in this country now, for all its past popularity. The ammunition companies don't see fit to provide the hunter with a very wide range of loads, and the sporting-goods dealers often don't bother to stock even those they do provide. For most of us, then, the 16-gauge has simply gotten squeezed to death between the heavy 20-gauge loads and the lighter 12-gauge fodder.

THE 20-GAUGE

The recent rise in popularity of the 20-gauge is a direct result of its shells being loaded to carry the same 1⅛ ounces of shot pellets used in target or field-loaded 12-gauge loads. But there are other factors involved. The manufacturers are now making the 20-gauge gun on a scaled-down, lightweight frame specifically designed for the gauge. Formerly, many American-made 20-gauge repeaters, whether pump or automatic, were built on the 12-gauge frame. Since the hunter carried practically the same weight and size gun as the big bore, he realized only the advantage of lighter recoil and suffered the disadvantage of many fewer pellets.

Now, the 20 is its own gun and as such has taken on a whole new personality. The lighter weight and smaller size afford excellent handling for the lady or beginning shooter of younger years and other gunners of less than average size or strength. Recoil is not severe, even in the heavy loads, and it's especially soft in the gas-operated autoloaders with their recoil retardant and damping effect. While giving longer shot strings than the 12, the 20-gauge 3-inch magnum is a potent performer on the marsh.

When used at the less-than-40-yard range normally encountered when shooting over decoys, the 20 should be considered quite adequate in the hands of those who know how to point it. But no matter how expert the shooter, nor how heavily loaded, the 20-gauge remains, at its very best, 10 yards less effective than a 12-gauge of the same loading. This is due to the longer shot string and the fact that any bore size, loaded with more shot than it was designed to handle, will invariably give a dense center pattern while becoming sparser at its outer perimeters, and place the center of its pattern and impact far lower than when shooting normal loads.

In spite of these shortcomings, the 20-gauge is becoming more popular, and in some respects is replacing the 12-gauge in much the same way and for the same reasons that the 12-gauge replaced the 10-gauge.

THE 10-GAUGE MAGNUM

Prior to 1900 the 12-gauge was considered too light for serious wildfowling. The 10-gauge was king of the duck guns. Then it was learned how to load 12-gauge shells that equaled, at least in shot weight, the standard 10-gauge load. Since then, we have seen the 12 replace the 10 to almost obscurity. An added push toward demise of the 10 was the discontinuance of most American-made double barrels and complete elimination of that gauge in the pump-action repeater, as well as its exclusion from trap-shooting competitions.

Starting in the late 1950s there was a sprinkling of overseas-made 10-gauge doubles reaching our shores; but they were, for the most part, crudely made, less than dependable, and, in some cases, of doubtful safety. They were sold as "goose" guns. Most were bored for the 3½-inch magnum shell, and their advertising attempted to assure the prospective buyer of take-home limits at any range. One importer used in his advertising a quote from one of America's finest gun handlers, "Dead ducks at 100 yards." It is possible to kill ducks at 100 yards, and having watched this man shoot, I have no doubt that he's done it. But it is farther than I care to shoot. The leads involved are fantastic, and the percentage

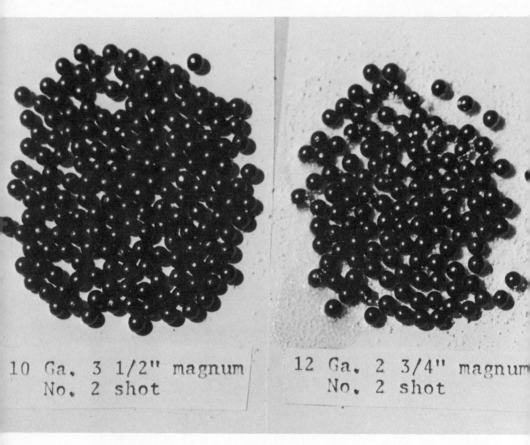

10 Ga. 3 1/2" magnum   12 Ga. 2 3/4" magnum
No. 2 shot   No. 2 shot

Many ducks are taken cleanly with 20-gauge and even smaller guns, but for my money the name of the game is shot, and the more, the better. Thus I consider the 10 gauge, which provides the most shot, the finest gauge there is for those who can handle it.

of ducks killed (not just hit) at this yardage is roughly that of lining up three bars on a slot machine.

So reappearance of the 10-gauge got off to a bad start. Its image was that of the long-range, far-out specialty gun. It was thought that those carrying it needed to be supermen to heft its heavy weight and stand up under the tremendous recoil. The awesome appearance of its giant shell discouraged many from even a trial firing. And the manufacturers of these shells gave you a wide choice of shot selection, providing you chose No. 2.

Arguments about the merits of the 10-gauge, pro or con, are few because it is, for the most part, little known and largely ignored. A pity, indeed, because even in its present limited availability of both guns and shells, it is actually our finest gauge for both duck and goose shooting.

First of all, recoil from a well-built, quality 10-gauge is neither deadly, devastating, nor even discomforting. With a weight of some 3 pounds more than the average 12-gauge duck gun, felt recoil of the big 3½-inch shell is little more, and sometimes less, than that of the 12-gauge magnum in lighter-weight guns. Actu-

How the 12-gauge (on the left) compares with the big 10. Beefed-up breeching provides the added weight needed to reduce felt recoil, along with making a very strong lock-up.

ally, it has more pleasant recoil—less sharp, and more a solid push than a kick. The usually longer and heavier barrels of the 10 give less whip than lighter 12s, making for faster recovery and steadying you down on target for a speedy second shot, and the stock dimensions of most 10s feature a butt width of ample size to spread recoil over a large area of the shoulder.

Ten to 12 pounds sounds like a lot of heft to push around on fast-moving targets. But if you're strong enough to lift it, you're strong enough to swing it; and once momentum has started, the gun is rock-steady in tracking the target, and the weight up forward of the heavy barrels makes it damn near impossible not to follow through.

Of course, the big 10 will not, by itself, fill the game bag of those who can't hit fairly well with the 12-gauge. But it does give the average "good" duck shot a definite advantage in cleanly killed birds at normal ranges.

The disadvantage of higher-priced shells can easily be overcome by purchasing a handloading kit like the very reasonably priced Lee Loader. If you take into consideration the fact that the average Midwestern duck hunter only expended thirty-six shells during a recent season, even the higher price of 10-gauge factory shells should not prove backbreaking for most.

With the appearance of better-made, yet reasonably priced, side-by-side double barrels, over and unders, and now a gas-operated autoloader, the big 10 should start receiving serious consideration for day-in, day-out duck hunting rather than being thought of as an oddity to extend the shotgun's range to its outer limits. If soft iron, or steel, shot is in our future for any length of time, the 10-gauge gun will *have* to receive serious consideration from the waterfowler.

Now that we've looked over the various gauges, let's give some consideration to the range of action types that are available.

THE SEMI-AUTOMATIC

Popularity of the autoloader is great among wildfowlers. The old arguments against its use have been pretty well invalidated by the modern waterproof plastic shell. The old paper hull was

The simple design of this Ithaca Model 51 gas-operated autoloader gives assurance of trouble-free operation.

prone to swell when wet or damp and would not always feed through the magazine and chamber when swollen. If it did chamber, often it would not extract. But now that the plastics have solved this problem, the only strike against the auto is in the minds of those who, like the British, think its use rather unsporting and in some ways equate it with a machine gun.

Whether it is operated by long recoil, short recoil, or gas, there are few malfunctions to be found in its shooting. Maintenance is minimal with the long-recoil system, requiring only proper placement of recoil rings for the load to be used, and the right kind of lubrication on the magazine tube. Oiling is of little worry today since almost all gun lubricants maintain the same viscosity over

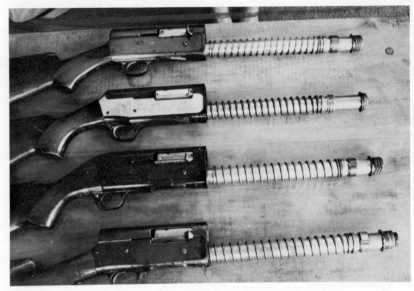

The Browning-type, long-recoil semi-automatic action is still popular and offered by several makers, but it is gradually giving way in numbers to more modern, shorter-recoil designs.

wide temperature ranges. There was a time when the Browning type of long-recoil-operated gun was thoroughly cleaned of all oils and lightly coated with kerosene for operation in subzero temperatures, while some employed heavy vaseline for use in very hot weather. Today, however, a wipe-off of old oil and any accumulated dirt and grit, and then a light spray or oily rag rub-down with modern lubricants, will give desired results under any range of temperature.

The gas-operated automatics require only an occasional chipping of the carbon from around gas ports and retaining ring. Today, most gas-operated models are designed to shoot high- or low-brass loads interchangeably. While it is your choice as to which type of action to choose, you might weigh the following:

The auto offers the duck hunter the advantage of an extra shell, compared with the double-barrel or over-and-under. No matter how many years you have used a pump gun, the auto will be

The most businesslike of sporting guns, the autoloader of today has lived down the reputation of being a fussy mechanism to keep in operation.

found quicker to use when you're bundled up in heavy clothing and shooting in off-balance positions. In my mind, it is the most efficient of duck guns.

THE PUMP GUN

The pump is a nearly century-old design that's changed little in its functional operation during its existence. The dedicated pump gunner is a hard man to talk into any other type of action. He enjoys being involved in the operation of his gun rather than being the captive of a mechanically programmed action, and he often figures that operating the pump helps his timing.

Our better models of slide-action guns are extremely reliable

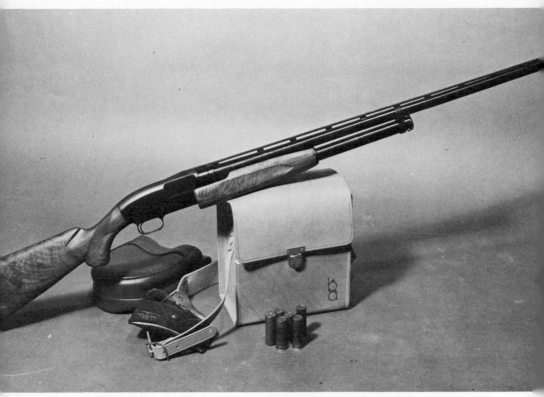

King of the pump guns, Winchester's Model 12 is once again a production gun, and a great favorite among duck hunters and trapshooters alike.

and have excellent balance and handling characteristics. They'll handle any shotgun fodder in almost any condition. Extraction is even more sure, positive, and strong than with the automatic; and in the hands of a man experienced in shooting this type of gun, there is little to be said against it. For the less experienced, however, the pump can offer problems in "short-chucking" if the gunner remembers to pump at all. This, of course, is the shooter's problem and does not reflect on the action itself.

Another advantage of the pump is its lower price. Gun for gun and quality for quality, a pump action may be had for less cost than an automatic or double-barrel. Its trigger pull can be adjusted to sharper let-off than present autos, and many models have a balance in the hands second only to fine doubles.

The classic duck gun, the side-by-side double, went into a long eclipse but is now making a strong comeback due to greater availability.

THE SIDE-BY-SIDE DOUBLE-BARREL

This is the traditionalist's gun. And he has many reasons for using it, some of which he is quick to expound upon, starting with the assertion that it's a "sportsman's" gun, that no more than two shots are needed in this day of short limits, that it is the highest attainment of the gunsmithing art—beautiful to behold and a pleasure to use.

More important, perhaps, is the double's advantage of instant choke selection. Doubles for wildfowling are usually bored with one tube full choke and the other modified, which gives you the right medicine for shooting both near and far birds. It can also handle any type of ammunition for which it is chambered, often an advantage under conditions where you prefer to use a light load in one barrel and, perhaps, a heavy goose load in the other. Finally, that the double-barrel inherently possesses the best balance of any type of shotgun is indisputable.

I believe the only reason we see so few side-by-sides in the blind today is the scarcity and cost of good-quality doubles. For many years, American production of the double gun has been at a near standstill because of our high manufacturing costs. However, we are now seeing many American brand names appear on medium-priced side-by-sides made overseas, and some are excellent buys indeed. More and more of them are being made along traditional double-gun lines and we will probably be seeing many more models appearing in the future.

For those who are used to them, double triggers are less costly and, in almost all cases, more reliable than the single-trigger models. Single triggers may be either selective or nonselective. You are able to choose which barrel to fire first with the selective trigger, which makes it even more expensive than the nonselective. It also makes it more prone to breakage and malfunction. This holds true whether it is operated mechanically or by recoil.

Despite this, there is much to be said for the single trigger's convenience for those unaccustomed to twin levers. Moreover, I've never shot a heavy-gauge double-triggered gun without experiencing the discomfort of a banged and bruised trigger finger, resulting from the kickback of the second trigger. Some authorities claim this is simply carelessness in holding the gun, but it's painful nevertheless. Some models get around this problem by making the front trigger fold forward on a hinge. It works to a degree, but you can still bruise your second finger against the rear of the trigger guard unless you keep a tight hold on the grip.

On big-gauge guns, especially the 10-gauge magnum, I have no sense of security with a single trigger because of its delicate mechanism and the heavy recoil. So while my choice would be a single selective trigger on a double for upland game and field use, I prefer two triggers on the large-gauge waterfowling gun.

THE OVER-AND-UNDER DOUBLE-BARREL

The over-and-unders became popular in America for general hunting in the early 1950s. Before that, most were found only in the hands of the live-bird, skeet, or trap shooters. Their cost was high and it has been only in the last few decades that we have seen good quality with a reasonable price tag.

The remarkable handling characteristics and great dependability of the Browning Superposed probably had more to do with

Fine balance and a single sighting plane are advantages offered by the over-and-under, though some complain that the deep barrel drop needed for loading and ejection is awkward in a cramped duck blind. This classy looking double is an Italian Gamba.

popularizing the type of action than any other gun. Its principal advantage is usually considered to be its single sighting plane, which is said to be less conducive to crossfiring than side-by-side tubes. Some nitpicky "experts," however, claim that stacked barrels are harder to handle in a crosswind, clumsier to handle during ejection and loading, and generally more awkward to use in the cramped quarters of a duck blind. My personal experience shows none of the above factors to be particularly significant. I've never given much thought to the matter, but have shot an over-and-under by preference for many years because of its good balance and handling and because I liked the gun.

Everything said about single triggers on the side-by-side double applies equally to the over-and-under. I use a single trigger by preference and have had malfunctions, but so few as to be negligible. And I enjoy the advantage of instant choice of choke, and the possibility of having two different types of shells ready for use.

THE 3-INCH CHAMBER

Some specialized duck guns are offered with longer chambers, suitable for the 3-inch magnum shell. This is usually done on guns of substantial weight, not because lighter guns would be unsafe with the 3-inch shell, but because their recoil would be severe. Browning beefs up its automatic in the recoil system to take this shell without giving undue punishment to the gun. Some of the gas-operated models are able to accept the 3-inch shell with only some juggling of the size of the gas ports and proper chambering. Break-action guns, both over-and-under and side-by-side, are also made with 3-inch chambers.

The 3-inch gun presents no problem, even in its heaviest weights, as a duck gun is seldom carried far; and most of us like a little heft in waterfowling guns, not only to reduce recoil but to help give stability in swinging and follow-through. The pros and cons of the shell itself are discussed in the next chapter.

BARREL LENGTH

Most magnum-chambered guns come with 30-inch barrels or longer, though it makes not a whit of difference in velocity or hitting power whether the barrel is 26 or 32 inches—with modern powder you get about what you will out of only 18 inches anyway. If you prefer a shorter-barreled gun for its faster handling, a 28-inch tube is not at all a bad choice. I don't object to the 30-inch, but feel anything beyond that is clumsy and unnecessary. The 26-inch barrels would be perfectly okay for close shooting over decoys, but most people like another couple of inches or more to give a longer, more precise sighting plane for long-range shooting.

SIGHTS

If I had to choose between a rib and a front sight, I would settle for the rib. Few seem to realize its importance in pointing a shotgun. There is no real use for a middle, or aligning, sight on a duck gun. If it's there, fine; leave it. But more importance should be placed on the front sight. Of course you've heard of someone losing his front sight and not missing it for weeks; but the fact remains, most of us do better shooting with some kind of front sight. If you're hunting in many areas with many types of backgrounds, one color may be as good as another. But if you have a more or less permanent shooting place, you may want to choose between the regular gold or white metal bead, as well as the ivory or fluorescent-red sights available today. The red color stands out particularly well against gray skies and over open water. I have found the ivory beads give good visibility against a tree-lined background whether in early-fall green or late-winter browns. It is against this latter type of background that a gold-colored bead often disappears completely. Many prefer a ramp front sight because its larger size is more quickly and easily seen. Under early-morning or late-evening conditions, the old-timer often used to wrap his muzzle in white adhesive tape. With shooting hours such as they are today, this now seems unnecessary.

Every few years someone re-invents a shotgun sight "that will revolutionize wing-shooting." There have been ring sights, tube sights, telescopic sights, and those that to the eye seemingly project a spot of light out on the target. Few have achieved lasting success over long periods, but perhaps this is because their inventors fail to credit wing-shooting as both an art and a science. The shotgun is not usually aimed at the target but where the tar-

An adjustable try-stock is a great aid in stock-fitting the experienced shotgunner whose gun-mounting pattern is well established, but not so practical for the beginner who never puts the gun up the same way twice.

get will be, and this, barring a fully computerized sighting system, means that the estimate of distance is up to the shooter. He already has two sets of sights to help in this estimation—the front sight, and his shooting eye which, with a shotgun, is the actual rear sight. That's all I've ever needed, but if something else helps you, go right ahead and use it.

STOCKS

Winter shooting with heavy clothing changes your stock fit, and may well make a stock too long. If the gun has a recoil pad, it can be replaced by a thin, solid-rubber butt plate which will shorten the pull by an inch or more, while the padding provided by your clothing should still keep recoil to a tolerable level.

Some hunters have two stocks for their gun, replacing the longer "mild-weather" stock with a shorter "cold-weather" stock. Others cut their regular stock short enough for winter hunting use, and then use a rubber slipover pad for use in warmer weather with less clothing. These are available at small cost from most any gun supply store. Unless you never shoot your duck gun except in season, you ought to make one of these adjustments.

SLINGS AND SWIVELS

Something that has amazed me for many years is the American duck hunter's total disdain for the sling strap on a shotgun. Slings are in general use throughout Europe, and almost all European shotguns not intended for export carry factory-installed swivels. The duck hunter often must carry lunch, decoys, shells, and extra clothing through swamp and marsh. All this while juggling his gun, too. Much easier, say I, to install a sling and toss the gun over your shoulder.

Swivels and slings are made to fit every American shotgun, as well as European. The cost is little and the convenience great.

CHOKE

In my book, *The Golden Age of Shotgunning* (Winchester Press) I gave a complete history of the shotgun choke, sorting out the claims and counterclaims of the many people who at one time or another were credited with its invention. I stated very honestly that I did not know who first discovered the choke, but suggested the credit should be given to Fred Kimble, an early Illinois duck hunter, who, so far as we know, was the first to bring it to public attention.

Choke boring as made known by Kimble and W. W. Greener must be ranked as one of the greatest discoveries in shooting. It improved the performance of the shotgun so much that one gun expert wrote, "When choke boring first came out, the man who had nothing better than cylinder was unhappy in the extreme. For the man with the choke gun was relentless, cruel, and so selfish that he lost no opportunity of displaying the marvelous performance of his improved weapon. The superiority of the chokebore was simply squelching."

It was choke boring that allowed the early market hunters to gain fame as marksmen. As early as the 1870s those professionals using choke-bored breechloaders were able to take ducks regularly at twice the distance normally thought possible by the cylinder-bored muzzleloader. But these early breechloaders were usually of large gauge, 8 and 10. They also produced patterns of uniformity not excelled to this date. And they used shells with such components as top wad, cork or fiber filler wads, and cardboard over powder wads, all of which we have eliminated as being detrimental to good patterns. Why this is so is another story. What we are concerned with here is how to achieve dense and even patterns at duck-gunning yardages.

The full choke probably represents 90 percent of the borings found on today's marsh. Its percentage would have been even higher a few years ago, but duck hunters are gradually learning that a more open bore not only gives better pattern percentages with large shot but also distributes the shot more evenly.

It has been said from the beginning of their general use that shot protectors, or collars, do not narrow patterns, but simply eliminate the "flyer" shot, bringing more shot into the pattern. My own testing and that of others whose knowledge I respect has not shown this to be entirely true. We find that shot collars do narrow your pattern; not appreciably so in some barrels, but very much so in others.

As Shotgun Editor of *Shooting Times* magazine, it has been my job for many years to test each new model of shotgun and evaluate it for our readers. I have shot literally thousands of test patterns, but still keep arriving back at the conclusion I reached when I first started to write on guns. In my experience, *patterns apply only to the particular gun and ammunition used to make them, and to no other.* Gun magazines frequently reproduce patterns obtained while testing new guns, but it is quite evident to me that these results are meaningless except for the particular gun that made them with the exact ammunition used. Therefore, it is up to the individual to make his own pattern tests to determine for himself what ammunition his gun handles best. This applies not only to brands of shells, but also most particularly to shot sizes.

Simply stated, we use a choke in a shotgun barrel for one reason. It is to put more pellets closer together in a smaller space than could be done without constricting the muzzle end of the barrel. A full-choke gun does not shoot any farther than a

No two barrels pattern alike. Most barrels put most of the shot in the center of the pattern, but note the open hole in the bottom of this one.

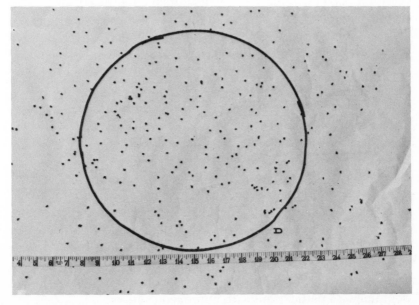

cylinder-bore, but at any yardage the full choke will put more shot into a given space.

Choke is obtained by making the inside diameter of the muzzle smaller than the rest of the barrel, and different makers use different methods. There are many types of choke, such as taper, swage, recess, and others. The way the manufacturer goes about doing this is not of concern here.

In America we have pretty well settled on three different degrees of choke. They are called improved cylinder, modified, and full. There are points in between, but the above three are standard on most factory guns. The degree of choke is measured in thousandths of an inch. A 12-gauge cylinder bore is .729 inch, while a full choke in the same gauge will measure about .693 inch. Even this may vary, since different gunmakers have different ideas as to what a full choke is. A good many European guns with full-choke markings are actually overchoked or overfull. And for any degree of choke marking we usually find the European guns smaller in diameter than those made in America. This is not as a rule desirable. Most barrels bored fuller than full choke deliver scattered and patchy patterns.

A truer way to judge the amount of choke is by the percentage of shot a barrel will place inside a 30-inch circle at 40 yards. This size of circle and distance has been used as a measure since the advent of choking. It makes a convenient standard of comparison. A 20-yard target would group the shot too close for easy counting and not allow distance enough for the shot to spread and give an accurate picture at normal ranges. A 60-yard target would introduce many variations besides being an unrealistic range for many gauges and loads. (About the only time we vary from the 40-yard target is in testing skeet guns and the .410-gauge, which is usually done at only 25 yards.)

Full-choke guns are supposed to place 65 to 75 percent of their shot charge within the circle; modified choke, 55 to 65; improved cylinder, 45 to 55; and true cylinder or skeet chokes, 35 to 45.

If I were to make a flat-out recommendation as to degree of choke giving best results for average duck hunting, I would have to say modified. The long-range pass-shooter would have a slight edge with full choke, and the man shooting birds over decoys would make a better score with improved cylinder.

Now ask me again: What is the ideal duck gun? One answer might be that it's a composite of all the guns we've just discussed, but I think that's cheating. I think the real answer is that it's the gun you shoot ducks best with. Some people tell you to buy any standard gun, more or less at random, and learn to shoot it. Some fine shots have been made that way, but I'd have to disagree with the advice. I'd suggest instead that you shop around and experiment a bit. It might take you a bit longer to find *your* ideal duck gun, but after all, that's half the fun!

4.
Duck Loads

Sooner or later most shooters come to favor a certain brand of shotshell, one that they secretly think shoots better than any other. Since confidence is a prime factor in wing-shooting, they should shoot that shell whenever possible. But as a practical matter, all American-made shotshells are pretty damn good, and there isn't much difference between them. Whether sold under national or proprietary brand names, most of the shells you can buy are manufactured by the same three or four manufacturers and are loaded to an accepted standard of performance.

You may choose one brand over another for many reasons—perhaps the color, perhaps a feeling that one brand of spent hull reloads better, or more times, than another; or a suspicion that a certain brand's wad configuration makes for better patterns or scfter recoil. The more advanced gunner may have determined to his satisfaction that a certain brand shoots better in his particular gun. But whatever brand you prefer, the fact is that you could pick up shells from your dealer's shelves with your eyes closed and still be assured of excellent performance in the field.

At the present stage of shotshell development there are many limitations. If we push velocity beyond our present loadings of

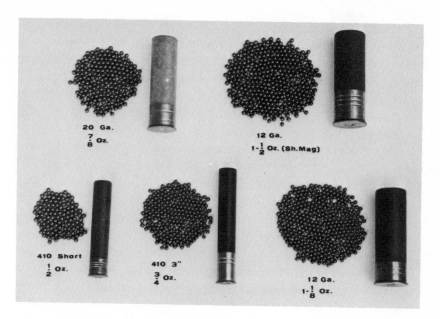

Just a quick glance at the amount of shot carried by the .410 shell indicates that it's no duck load, even in the hands of an expert.

1300 to 1400 fps, we reach diminishing returns by blowing patterns. (This is a factor many handloaders overlook when turning out their "hotter-than-factory" stuff.) But bless the basement ballistician who works carefully and follows closely the published data recommended by reputable firms. He can turn out excellent tailor-made fodder and enjoy the self-satisfaction that comes from "shooting your own," not to mention the savings in money.

When making a choice of loads you must first determine the conditions under which you will be shooting. The chap who waits his birds out and only lets fly at those in range will do quite well with regular low-brass field or target loads of 1⅛ ounces, shot in 12-gauge. Such shells cost less money, produce less recoil, and won't mutilate birds taken close to the gunner. (Because of the shorter range you can use smaller shot and more open chokes and still retain enough pattern density and impact energy per pellet.)

Sometimes, however, this same patient type of hunter may find that the birds aren't working too well, and perhaps are only

skirting the edges of his blocks. Under these conditions he needs
a bit more whomp, and can easily elect to use high-brass Express
loads of somewhat greater velocity and carrying more pellets per
copy. With 1¼ ounces of shot, he can still use smaller shot sizes
such as No. 6 or 7½ for pattern density, and still retain adequate
energy if he doesn't try to reach out beyond 40 yards.

The pass shooter who must take his birds at ranges over 50
yards or never pop a cap has another set of problems. To him,
the key factor is shot—the more the better within recognized
limits. This means not only high-brass loads but larger shot sizes,
and preferably in the king-size loadings we call "magnum."
Magnum shells not only carry more shot, they also cost more
money and kick harder. Magnums come both in the standard
2¾-inch length, which can be safely used in the normally chambered gun, and the heavier-loaded 3-inch shell, which requires a
specially chambered barrel and usually a beefed-up action. Many
of us consider the long shell with its longer shot string a ballistic

*Comparison of the amount of shot contained in the three standard 20-gauge
duck loads: 3-inch magnum, short magnum, and regular field load.*

bastard and prefer results obtained from the shorter maggie, but the fact remains that the 3-incher carries the greatest shot load available in 12-gauge. Both regular and 3-inch magnums are in the "overkill" class for shooting over decoys, but can provide the added edge needed to reduce crippling in downrange shooting.

The hunter has little choice in the amount and kind of powder the factory packs in its shells, for it's always so many drams equivalent of smokeless powder. (Why we are still using "drams equivalent" is beyond me. It means that the amount of modern smokeless powder in the shell would be roughly equal to the stipulated weight of black powder, and thus provides a scale of comparison. However, I doubt that many of today's hunters have enough black-powder experience to appreciate the comparison or care about it.) In any event, the powder charge is marked right there on the shell box, so you have at least some idea of what kind of blast to expect. And as we say, since your choice is pretty limited, it is probably all the information you need. Not so with shot size selection.

PELLET SIZE

You may be sure that a certain size of shot gives better results, but even the fellow sharing your blind may disagree with the choice.

American shot has been manufactured in sizes ranging from a solid ball the size of the bore to "dust" which weighs out around

	Shot Size	No. of Shot per Ounce
•	9	585
•	8	410
●	7½	350
●	6	225
●	5	170
●	4	135
●	2	90
●	BB	50

COMPARATIVE SHOT SIZES (ACTUAL SIZE)

4,500 *pellets* to the ounce. However, No. 12 is about as small as we find today and its use is limited mostly to .22 shot cartridges. Size BB is the largest factory-loaded lead birdshot in use today and the ammo makers have wisely dropped No. 1 as redundant. I've never missed it, and I can live without No. 7 as well.

However, I do regret not being able to grab store-bought shells with No. 3 stuffings. A careful check of the figures and my own experience leads me to believe the long-range duck and goose shooter needs more pellets per ounce than are offered by No. 2 and more impact than he gets from No. 4. There is talk of making No. 3 loaded shells again, but don't wear leaky boots until you get 'em.

Generally, though, there is no reason why the seven or eight different lead shot sizes now available shouldn't be adequate for all our gunning needs, if we understand what is needed. But therein lies a problem; too few gunners today down enough game to determine empirically what performs best.

The ammo makers periodically publish charts suggesting the best sizes of shot to use for certain types of game. They usually recommend something like "No. 2 and No. 4 for geese," etc. Some are more definitive, breaking down the general heading of "ducks" into canvasback, sprig, teal, and so forth, ad infinitum. These charts are a definite help to the beginning or occasional shooter, and any of the recommended shot sizes are suitable for the intended species under certain conditions. Nonetheless, it is hard to design a chart that can give complete answers, taking

PELLET ENERGY AT MUZZLE AND AT HUNTING RANGES

Pellet energy in ft. lbs.   *Muzzle velocity 1250 f.p.s.*

size shot	muzzle	20 yds	40 yds	60 yds
No. 2	16.75	10.60	7.25	5.40
No. 4	11.05	6.65	4.45	3.20
No. 5	8.80	5.05	3.30	2.35
No. 6	6.65	3.70	2.35	1.65
No. 7½	4.30	2.20	1.35	0.90
No. 8	3.70	1.80	1.05	0.70

all variables into consideration. But while the charts are an excellent guideline, they can be even more helpful when we add our own "uncharted" set of conditions. Probably the most important of these are gauge, choke, and the range at which game is to be taken.

Certainly the most important of these factors is range. In end result, it makes little difference to a bird whether he is centered with No. 2s or 7½s at 25 yards; he's a goner. But when we stretch out to 40 yards and beyond, there is a great deal of difference— the difference between a lost cripple and a clean, ground-thumping kill. Out there we need all the help we can get, and need to be more choosy in the selection of shot.

First of all, it helps to understand the basic characteristics of different sizes of shot and forget our own personal preference and prejudices. These are too often based on lucky hits, local custom, or bad advice. For the moment, forget what you've heard about 7½s for head shots on geese, and 2s preventing shot-up birds.

Primarily, two things are demanded of shot. One, it must have the mass to maintain velocity and reach the target with at least 1½ foot-pounds per pellet of remaining energy. This is the minimum amount needed to drive through bone and feathers to a vital area in the bird. Secondly, there must be three to five of these pellets entering the body for a clean and certain knockdown.

Range, again, is the principal influencing factor. A look at the pellet energy chart will show that all sizes from No. 2 through No. 8 have enough shocking force at 20 yards. At 40 yards we must disqualify 7½ and 8. Add another 20 yards and No. 6 barely makes it. Beyond that, damn few birds are killed with any size shot except by the most expert gunners or the most bald-faced liars.

Using the 1½ foot-pound minimum, it becomes apparent that long yardage calls for large shot. But here we run into trouble, because the larger the pellets the fewer of them in any given load, and we still need enough pattern density to put three to five of them on target.

Even in the heavy 12-gauge, 3-inch magnum load of 1⅞ ounces of No. 2 shot there are only 169 pellets. And even the tightest of full chokes will produce patterns with holes 3 to 4 inches across at 60 yards. The vital area of a duck measures about the same, so it becomes a matter of luck rather than gunning skill to place multiple pellets of No. 2 on target. So we must compromise. We can obtain an additional 85 pellets and still be above minimum shocking power by going to No. 4 in the same load. The odds improve visibly in our favor with the tighter pattern.

However, gauge and choke must also enter into judgment. Those shooting 16- and 20-gauge guns may find that even No. 4 gives too few pellets, and must weigh this against using even smaller shot with less impact.

The heavy 20-gauge load of 1¼ ounces carries the same number of No. 4 pellets as the 1⅞-ounce 12-gauge maggie load does of No. 2—169 pellets. So unless you are trying to stretch your 20 beyond its proper limits, you would be better off using No. 6 shot with its greater number of 281 pellets, despite their lesser energy.

Without belaboring the point, I think the preceding example says something of the futility of using gauges smaller than 20 at long range. There is just no getting around the fact that a good big gun will beat a good little gun.

After many years of shooting patterns, literally thousands of them, I am convinced that full-choke barrels do not, on the average, give as even a distribution of large-size shot as more open barrels. Almost any full choke from a reputable maker today will print acceptably with No. 6 shot and smaller. In fact, I cannot recall having ever tested a full-choke barrel that did not give

APPROXIMATE NUMBER OF LEAD PELLETS PER LOAD

Shot Size	BB	2	4	5	6	7½
Ozs. shot 1⅞	93	168	252	318		
1⅝	81	146	219	276	366	
1½		135	203	256	337	
1⅜	69	124	186		309	
1¼	63	113	169	213	281	438
1⅛		101	152	191	253	394
1		90	135	170	225	350

good or better patterns with 7½s. But the majority of full chokes seem to get patchy from No. 4 on up.

My best patterns with large-size shot have always been made with modified or improved/modified barrels. Even skeet chokes handle No. 4s with fine distribution, and serve splendidly for geese over decoys.

So it is not enough to pattern your gun with one size of shot only. You must experiment with different sizes until you find what best suits your individual barrel and choking, while keeping in mind both game and the range at which it will be shot. Fortunately we have a definite advantage today over the hunters of even a few short years ago. Today's shells employ a protective plastic shot collar that helps to prevent deformed shot, and puts back into the pattern pellets that would otherwise have become "flyers" due to deformation. In other words, you obtain the effect of a tighter choke in terms of density of pattern.

Once we've gotten down to this fine a point, the choice of loads becomes a personal matter between the shooter, his gun, and gunning conditions. Only you know the type of game and at what yardage most shots will be made. Then if you add in the possibility of winds that may take heavier shot to buck, and velocity of the shell to be used, the charts will give a pretty good indication of the size shot needed and what you can expect from it. If you still need a "rule of thumb," just remember this: *Always*

RECOMMENDED SHOT SIZES (LEAD SHOT)

GEESE

Pass shooting, 12, 16 or 20 gauge	No. 2
Pass shooting, 3½-inch 10-gauge magnum	BB or No. 2
Over decoys	No. 2 or No. 4

BIG DUCKS

Pass shooting	No. 4
Over decoys	No. 4, 5 or 6

SMALL DUCKS

Pass shooting	No. 5 or No. 6
Over decoys	No. 6 or No. 7½

choose the smallest size shot that affords the minimum energy
needed at the longest yardage you intend to shoot.

How does this work out in practice? The long experience of
many hunters yields the following guidelines:

Even in pass shooting, nothing larger than No. 4 should be
used on ducks. Over decoys, No. 5 or 6, or even 7½, will give
best results. Nothing smaller can be recommended unless you
enjoy paddling after cripples. Range is the determining factor.
However, a few loads of No. 7½ or 8 kept in a separate pocket
of your hunting coat are handy for dispatching a downed but
still lively bird. (Once a bird is on the water, there is little to
hope for except a head shot, and the smaller pellets improve
the odds.)

I've never seen a legitimate use for BB shot in wildfowling,
and believe the figures support me. There are only 50 pellets
per ounce—certainly not nearly enough when spread out in your
pattern at long range. Random pellets can break wings, but seldom give a clean kill at yardage. I'm told that BBs are a good
choice for fox, which is a bigger target, but my experience in
that type of hunting is too limited to justify an opinion.

Going by the figures, it would seem No. 2 is the largest shot
that should be used for geese under any conditions. It is surely
the most popular among the Canada goose hunters who shoot
on controlled shooting areas and daily-fee clubs, but even they
would perhaps be better armed with the denser patterns of No. 4.

Round shot is not the best of all shapes ballistically, but it is
the best we have found, all things considered. Similarly, lead
is not the best material in many respects, either, though it may
also be the best we've found to date. Currently, however, a lot
of work is being done to find a suitable substitute.

IRON SHOT

As this is published we are confronted with a problem we've
recognized for over a hundred years but only recently have
started to do much about: loss of our waterfowl directly due
to lead poisoning through ingested shot. The poisoning is due to
eaten, not imbedded, shot. In other words, the hunter never
need touch the bird—the damage is done by his shot pellets

lying on the bottoms of our sloughs and marshes. The shot is picked up by the birds along with grit and weed seeds of similar size and shape.

This occurs chiefly in spots where the banks and bottoms are hard enough so that shot doesn't sink quickly—and where so much shooting is done that a significant number of pellets will be present. Obviously, such areas aren't sufficiently typical for an easy or reliable count of ducks killed (or poisoned but not yet dead) as a result of ingesting lead. There are no hard figures, just widely ranging guesses and estimates, some ranging higher than a million birds per year.

To eliminate this, our ammunition companies have experimented for many years to find a suitable nontoxic substitute for lead. This experimentation has been accelerated tremendously the last few years, and truly extensive tests and research have been conducted. The only material so far found at all promising is iron—and iron is *most* promising in combination with lead.

The first attempts at "steel," or soft iron, proved the pellets would age-harden to the point of grooving gun barrels. This has been improved upon, but iron is still potentially damaging to some barrels, especially the thin, soft tubes of fine-quality double guns. So iron (or steel) is not really a suitable substitute for lead; rather, it is the only substitute we have found.

On first acquaintance with the problem you can no doubt think of hundreds of logical substitutes for lead. But over the years scientists and technologists have tried and tested a mind-boggling number of substances and compounds. However, the grinding action of the gizzard and the hydrochloric acid of the duck's stomach have confounded efforts to use shot plated with any known material, metal or plastic. Solid copper appeared promising until it was found to be just as lethal as lead, though acting far more slowly. As early as 1936 an effort was made to formulate a lead/magnesium alloy that would melt away. Hundreds of other compounds of tin, antimony, and what-have-you have been tried and abandoned. The Illinois Institute of Technology even spent two years trying to perfect a water-soluble shot.

Since ducks can pick shot from only the top few inches of bottom, it has been suggested that we use only large, heavy shot, which will sink sufficiently on soft bottoms. But this solution, of course, can apply only to certain areas. Another thought is to cover shot-laden bottoms with pea gravel, an idea that might work in some places, but would be impossible in many others, since some 70 million acres of our country are involved. Yet even if lead shot were banned today, it would take many years for contaminated areas to cleanse themselves, so steel shot can hardly be the only answer.

Since it does not poison our waterfowl, why don't we just accept iron as a substitute for lead shot? So far as I am concerned, the weakest argument against the use of iron is the fact that it costs roughly 2½ times as much as lead. Few of us have ever considered duck hunting an inexpensive sport, and even fewer dedicated duck hunters would consider a shell increase of $3 (or even $30) a box exorbitant if we could save a million or so ducks per year. In view of the fact the average Midwestern duck hunter is said to shoot only thirty-six shells per season, the additional cost would be small.

Damage to the shotgun barrel itself through use of iron was first thought extensive, and there are tests around to prove that it is, on older guns. However, other tests show no discernible damage to the choke from peening action of the harder shot, and no grooving of the barrels on modern production guns. Some older guns have shown ringing or bulging around the forcing cone, so it is generally concluded that damage could occur in fine old guns with thin soft-steel barrels. In other words, it may be best not to risk your Purdey or Parker by using iron shot.

We now reach the crux of the controversy—crippling. This is, and has been, the major issue. It is the primary reason the ammo industry has been blamed for dragging its feet and not getting into full production of iron-shot loads. Nobody can argue that, size for size, iron is less dense and lighter than lead. It will not buck wind or maintain momentum and impact to the same degree as the heavier lead. Early in the game, it was found that iron had to be upped two shot sizes over lead to deliver comparable foot-pounds of energy. Using a standard 2¾-inch shell, this meant fewer pellets per load, meaning fewer pellets on target due to a sparser pattern, and seeming to suggest a 30- or 40-yard limit for sure kills with iron. But the most recent tests made under tightly controlled conditions seem to both confirm and deny this. Moreover, newer types of powders and more efficient wadding are enabling the industry to pack more pellets in the standard-size shotgun shell.

Nevertheless, the most thorough test so far published indicates that, in bagging ducks at between 40 and 80 yards, No. 4 iron shot crippled from 2.5 to 4.3 times as many as lead shot. This study concluded from figures derived elsewhere that the use of iron shot would increase crippling by more than 3 million birds. Yet another test conducted by another company showed that among birds hit using No. 4 iron, 15.4 percent were downed, but lost, which when projected on a national scale showed a crippling loss of about 800,000 birds. Still other estimates run from "no additional loss" up to and including 1 million.

Even though an exact or even approximate number cannot be agreed upon, informed opinion overwhelmingly concludes that the mandatory use of iron will result in greater crippling loss than we now suffer from lead. However, at present we may be losing approximately the same number of birds from lead poisoning (2 to 3 percent) as we do from crippling (2½ percent)—or a total estimate of more than 5 percent loss from both causes.

I've experimented with iron shot for the past two duck seasons in several states, but only to the extent of six boxes of shells. With the amount of scientific research already conducted, my personal opinion is somewhat irrelevant and I'll limit it to simply commenting that when using iron shot at reasonable ranges, I seemed to score neither better nor worse than I have in the past with standard shells. A load of 1⅛ ounces of No. 4 iron and 1¼ ounces of No. 6 lead can be loaded to the same muzzle velocity of 1330 fps. At 40 yards the iron shot has slowed only 36 fps more than lead and its individual pellet energy is 0.7 foot-pound higher.

You use the same lead on crossing birds, and the percentage of a 40-yard pattern in the standard 30-inch circle is equivalent, but of course not as dense since the iron load carries 58 fewer pellets.

I noticed no gun or barrel damage whatsoever, which is hardly a scientific observation. Possibly because of the very light recoil from the iron loads, plus that I was aware I was not tossing as much shot, the new shells did little to instill confidence. This may or may not have contributed to my poorer-than-usual results on birds at 50 or more yards.

No one I've talked with *likes* to shoot iron shot. No one has proved to us that its adoption will save a great many birds when we balance out crippling versus poisoning. Probably the only way we'll find out is to test it in the field under actual conditions by a large number of hunters over a wide area for a lengthy period.

At the time of this writing, the Canadian Wildlife Service is studying the effects of shot pellets that combine powdered lead and iron. The pellets are sintered to increase density (by eliminating the tiny spaces between metal particles). It has been found that a pure corn diet increases the danger of lead poisoning, yet studies indicate that pellets containing 25 percent lead are nontoxic to mallards dosed with eight pellets and kept on a corn diet for 120 days! There isn't enough lead in such pellets for optimum ballistics, but tests show that pellets with 50 percent lead are only slightly toxic—and much better ballistically. Ducks dosed with four of these pellets survived a 48-day corn diet in excellent condition. Thus, while further research is necessary, we can conclude that one new approach holds great promise.

5.
How to
Drop a Duck

By rights, we probably ought to proceed from guns and loads to the rest of the duck hunter's equipment—blinds, boats, calls, and tactics—before dealing with the business of how to knock down ducks. However, there's also a certain logic to proceeding from guns and loads to how to use them. In addition, for most hunters this will probably be one of the more interesting chapters, and it's certainly an important one, for you're not much of a duck hunter if you can't hit a reasonable proportion of the birds you shoot at.

As a starter, what is a reasonable ratio of hits to misses? That's a tricky question. The great market hunters like Fred Kimble ran long strings of ducks without missing, and even the ordinarily competent trap or skeet shot ought to average pretty well over decoys when the ducks are stooling well. On the other hand, I've never seen anyone who didn't have his hit and miss days, and on difficult pass shooting, even veterans often expend four to six shells for every duck bagged. I suppose the truest statement of all is that in shotgunning, a hit is history and a miss is a mystery.

In short, the beginner shouldn't expect something to drop from the sky every time he trips the trigger. Even gunners who have achieved some proficiency in other forms of wing-shooting will probably find that they average lower on ducks, due to harder conditions and longer ranges.

The many good books and articles that have been written on how to shoot a shotgun all stress the importance of correct basic stance, gun mounting, and swing, and they're right. The trouble is that as a wildfowler you'll seldom find it possible to choose your posture. You have to take what you can get.

Most duck shooting is done under adverse, if not deplorable, conditions. You are often required to shoot off balance, body twisted, gun canted. Your hands are cold and eyes runny. That

The camera shot this flock of pintails en masse, and the shotgunner is often tempted to think he can do the same. Don't you believe it; flock-shooting produces poor results, and it's always better to concentrate on one bird.

smooth swing and follow-through recommended by the books will be restricted by brush, blind, and bulky clothing. You may be knee-deep in mud, fighting for balance in a rocking boat, or precariously perched on a muskrat house; you may be shooting from your knees, or lying on your back. To further complicate matters, you are shooting at unknown ranges and unpredictable angles in dim light, heavy wind, and perhaps driving rain or snow.

So the duck hunter quickly finds that he must set aside much of what he has been taught of the classic styles of shooting and develop a whole new type of gunnery.

The accomplished duck shot uses all three methods of leading a target—snap shooting, swing-through, and sustained lead. He must use all three or otherwise pass up many shots too difficult for a single style of shooting. It is said that 90 percent of the ducks are taken by 10 percent of the hunters. I accept this, since the veteran shooter may fill his bag from shots the newer man wouldn't dare attempt. The good duck shot knows how to use all methods of gun pointing from any body position.

SNAP SHOOTING

Snap shooting is a rapid reckoning as to where the bird will be when your shot reaches it. You quickly throw gun to shoulder and fire without hesitation. You form a "sight picture" with no time for a conscious lead. It is an instinctive type of aiming, useful on fast or quickly disappearing targets at close range. Some of you shoot this way now and can no doubt wipe out most of us on quail or walked-up grouse in timber, but may find you don't score so well at longer yardages.

The snap shot is useful in taking the first bird of a pair in jump shooting and perhaps when a sneaky but speedy greenwing teal buzzes your blind, heading for nearby cover. It is often the only type of lead you can use in small clearings or for taking birds through holes in the tree-tops. It may be all the aiming time you have when trying for a double or triple kill.

SWING-THROUGH

The swing-through is the most frequently used method of leading medium-range targets. It is done by rapidly coming from be-

This mallard drake has just shifted gears, and is getting the hell out of there! You won't have time to point him out, and a fast swing-through with a generous amount of lead is the only way you'll ever nail him with any frequency.

hind the target while tracking its line of flight, then pulling the trigger as the gun reaches and swings past it. The slowness of your reaction time and the speed of your swing supposedly take care of the amount of lead required, and your sense of timing can become very acute with practice. This method is much used by trapshooters and has probably accounted for more game than the other two types of lead combined. It is the way you'll take the majority of ducks over decoys, and its only real drawback is in requiring practice to be effective. Timing must be developed and maintained through regular shooting, and those casing their shotgun eleven months of the year may find themselves a bit rusty on opening day.

Pass shooting usually involves a sustained lead, and requires a better judgment of leads than any other form of wildfowling. Figures don't mean much, but most novices never hit anything until they start doubling their "normal" leads.

SUSTAINED LEAD

Often called "pointing out," a sustained lead means you get in front of your target and stay there. You compute the speed of the bird, as well as its angle of flight, wind, and yardage. If this works out in your mind to 6 or 8 feet of lead, you point your muzzle that far ahead of the bird and maintain that distance by swinging with the bird until *after* pulling the trigger.

Sustained lead is a tool for the long-range expert who undoubtedly became one from a lot of long-range shooting. So again, don't expect too much when starting out. Telling someone to "give it 6 feet" means little or nothing. If all variables are known (and they never are), mathematical lead *could* be figured with exact certainty; but you wouldn't have time to do it anyway. Lead is an approximation, differing with the experience, reaction time, and judgment of the individual.

ESTIMATING RANGE

Ask five men to select a mark 50 yards away and you'll get five different answers. Accurate estimation of range is rare—even more so over water, or when involving height. Some hunters use helpful gimmicks such as sticks set at 10- or 20-yard intervals from the blind. Others claim that when you can see their color, birds are close enough. Most of us depend on the image size of the bird, but it can be a deceptive method. Every hunter has watched approaching ducks by peeking through parted brush, but when standing to shoot found they were still to hell and gone out of range.

Alas, I know of no shortcuts to even fairly exact rangefinding. After having looked at a lot of birds for many years, I'm still

This dropping duck, still more than fifty yards away, will probably flare upwards when he spots the hunter, even during the shot charge's flight time. Shooters must learn to anticipate where the duck will be by the time the shot reaches that range.

uncertain of distance more times than not. But I am sure that many of your proud 70-yard kills were in reality closer to fifty.

SPEED OF FLIGHT

Flight speed is another guessing game. An old Canada goose flies as fast as a mallard (both can do 60 miles an hour), but doesn't appear to. The big canvasback with his steady flight of 70-plus mph is the speed king and looks it, but the small darting teal actually moving 15 to 20 mph slower appears almost as fast. You should also remember that all species have both a cruising and an escape speed. Birds peacefully drifting into the decoys can really turn it on when shot at.

Simply to offer the beginning shooter some inkling of a duck's speed and the lead required, let's lump together mallards, black ducks, pintails, and woodies. All can fly between 50 and 90 feet per second with normal flight averaging around 70 fps (over 45 mph). This means a crossing flight at 40 yards calls for 4 or 5 feet of sustained lead. With teal, wigeon, and gadwall you tack

AVERAGE FLIGHT SPEEDS OF DIFFERENT WILDFOWL

Speed of average flight in *feet per second.*

Black Duck	70
Mallard	70
Spoonbill	65
Pintail	75
Wigeon	75
Wood Duck	70
Gadwall	75
Teal	85
Redhead	85
Bluebill	85
Canvasback	95
Canada Goose	80
Snow Goose	80

This looks like a triple in the making, but watch the drake in the middle—

on another foot, and another yet for canvasback. Again, this is said only in the belief that some idea is better than none at all.

HIGH WIND

No sooner has the new shooter learned to lead and connect with some regularity under ordinary conditions than he hunts on a day of high wind and hits nothing.

Have you ever taken dead aim at a cripple on the water only to have the wind blow your pattern a couple of feet away from the bird? The same thing happens with ducks in flight. If you are shooting high-brass shells, No. 4 shot, with a muzzle velocity of 1330 fps in a 30-mph crosswind, you can expect your pellets to drift 15 inches at 40 yards and nearly twice that at 60. When using smaller No. 6 pellets, add another foot of drift to the above figures. Program an additional 10 mph of wind, and you can add still an additional foot. The shot charge is now hitting 4 feet off your aiming point when using No. 4 lead shot. The lighter-weight iron shot, at its present state of development, must be upped two full shot sizes for it to be comparable. These figures assume you are shooting in a 90-degree crosswind; of course, shot drift is less in a quartering wind.

This may be the place to state that you gain little in wind-bucking ability from high-velocity loads at yardage. High-brass

he might side-slip right out of your pattern!

loads poop out to nearly target-load speed within the first 40 yards by having to overcome greater air resistance at their greater speed. No. 4 shot starting at the muzzle with 1200 fps has slowed to about 650 fps at 60 yards. The same shot starting at 1350 fps will only be going 35 fps faster. Add to the above an estimation for the gravity drop of shot, and all these figures will tell you something of the problems facing those who fancy themselves long-range specialists.

PRACTICE

Those buying their first gun and intending to learn how to use it have only one choice today, for there are no longer opportunities for enough practice to learn wing-shooting in the field. The new or not-so-proficient gunner will do well to consider skeet or trap shooting. While claybirds will not make him a great duck shot, they do offer the speediest and most pleasurable way of starting in that direction. Skeet clubs are found in or near any larger metropolitan area, and trapshooting is so widespread that it can be found a short drive from almost any town or village.

The average duck hunter counts a season ordinarily busy if he goes through two or three boxes of shells. This is hardly a weekly average for those interested in the claybird sports. Trap and skeet allow shooting enough shells in a short time to thoroughly familiarize you with your gun, so that you can forget its function and concentrate on hitting. You learn basic gun handling, how to lead, and, most importantly, develop confidence in your ability to hit a moving target. You also associate with more experienced shooters who can pass on their knowledge and ways of gun handling.

Many duck hunters use regular skeet and trap as a before-season warm-up. Others find a strong-armed buddy with a handtrap. The handtrap can toss targets closely approximating many difficult shots presented during actual duck hunting. The trapper can stand to one side behind you, perhaps in a gully or on a hill. He can throw birds at all angles and heights, through small openings in trees, or otherwise give you practice on rapidly disappearing targets. The shooter can try different positions, perhaps sitting or crouching behind brush. Handtrap practice is limited only by your imagination.

Considering all aspects of wing-shooting, practice is by far the most vital requirement. I've had the privilege of shooting with many of the world's best—men who have made their reputation in the live-bird ring, at claybirds, or in the game fields. I've studied, photographed, and written about them but have discovered only three things they share in common. All are competitive by nature, have good powers of concentration, and shoot an awful lot of shells. In my opinion you cannot be a consistently good wing shot unless you frequently practice shooting.

WATCH THE BIRDIE

The secret of great game gunnery (if such exists) can be summed up in three words—"watch the birdie." Simple as it sounds, the idea is hard to get across to new shooters as well as many old-timers. But I'm convinced that most shooters of average ability can double their hits on waterfowl by carefully observing what the bird is doing, and anticipating what it is about to do. In other words, try to see more than just a moving object beyond the front sight of your gun. Many gunners sense only a blurred image, heading a certain direction at a given speed. The clever gunner sees much more.

As an example, let's consider a high mallard coming dead on toward you but rapidly losing elevation to set in your decoys. The normal lead would be directly beneath him, an amount commensurate with his speed of approach. But if you watch carefully, he's not coming directly in. Rather, he is pitching, turning, sideslipping, and correcting balance by coordinating tail, wings, and body according to air currents. The amount of sideslipping can be a full pattern spread in a fresh wind. If you notice it, you can correct for it.

Now assume it's the same bird, but he sees you rise from cover

This is a difficult shot, since little body area is presented. Rather than take this shot, it would be better to wait, or to make the birds flare or turn so they produce a larger target.

This bird has spotted something amiss, and his widened tail and outstretched wings are preliminary to evasive action.

to take him. He'll flare, and it will be telegraphed by a widely opened tail and fast-flapping wings to check his descent. This is your tip-off to shorten your lead. While he can't correct or terminate his fall instantaneously, he will considerably slow his speed

The claybird sports of skeet and trap make an excellent pre-season warm-up, and provide the best opportunity, in these days of limited bags, for the average hunter to become thoroughly familiar with his gun.

of descent, and you will lead him too far underneath unless you anticipate his action.

These are only two examples of the infinite possibilities you learn to recognize by paying close attention to a bird's flight pattern and marking clues to flight changes before he makes them. Knowing how a bird may react and how his flight pattern may change gives you the split-second edge you need to change with him.

6.
Wildfowling
Ways and Weather

WEATHER

The ways of duck and goose hunting cover a vast amount of territory, literally and figuratively, and no one man in one lifetime could hope to have hunted it all, or know all the ways to hunt it. About the only common denominator that applies to all areas and all types of wildfowling is the weather. It's not always the same, but it's always there. And since ducks seem to be able to anticipate changing weather at least as well as the average graduate meteorologist, the duck hunter learns to keep a "weather eye" for fronts coming through, and suffers a private hell if unable to get to the marsh when they occur. He pays unusual attention to forecasts because he knows that fronts moving in are usually accompanied by ducks moving in, as much as twelve to twenty-four hours ahead of the weather.

This activity means "new" ducks. They will be "working" birds, readily decoying to even stale decoy sets the resident birds have long learned to avoid. Such fronts may even signal the "grand "passage" or mass migration of the bulk of the ducks left in Far Northern territory. Vast flocks may have flown all night and at dawn can be seen folding their wings and dropping rock-fast from

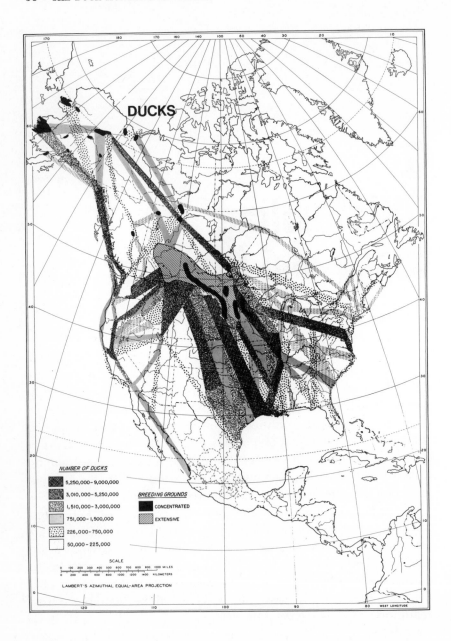

DUCK MIGRATION CORRIDORS
Courtesy Frank C. Bellrose, Illinois Natural History Survey

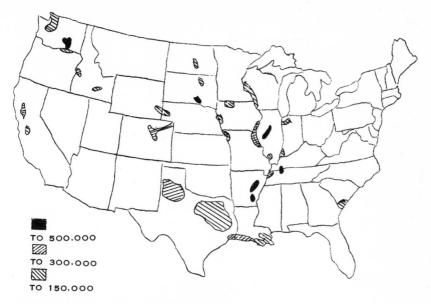

AREAS OF MALLARD CONCENTRATION IN MIGRATION
Major areas of peak density during the fall migration

high altitude to centers of wide water. There they'll raft and rest. Soon they will break into smaller groups to search for food and shelter. It is then your decoys and duck call pay the greatest dividends.

There are few instructions to be given for hunting under these circumstances, and even fewer needed. It's a period of fine hunting. It won't last long, but while it does it will make up for the many dry, duckless days we all experience.

Solunar tables predicting the periods of greatest activity among wildlife are often surprisingly accurate. No one seems able to prove exactly why, but it is thought to have to do with barometric or atmospheric pressure, phases of the moon, and some of the other subtle natural forces thought by some to affect human behavior, too.

Whatever the reason, the duck hunter must pay strict attention to weather forecasts, as even mild fronts mean wind, and wind means movement of waterfowl. Any wind gives you a chance to plan decoy placement, plot direction from which birds will approach, and decide best which shore to shoot.

Wind

High winds force the birds to seek shelter; the gale-force winds accompanying storm systems cause them to lose their natural wariness and put them at a decided disadvantage. In such winds you may see geese overhead no more than 20 yards high attempting to fly into the wind, but standing still or losing ground until they tire, flip over on outstretched wings, and reverse direction with tremendous speed.

Duck-hunting weather? It certainly can be, but only if the hunter knows how to call the ducks in to where he can see them.

Rain

If you've ever heard the warning, "You can't kill mallards in the rain," forget it! Some of the best mallard shoots I can recall were on days when a warm, misty, but steady rain was falling and the old greenheads ended up working just as if it had been bright and beautiful. However, they may spend a long time sittin' before deciding to work. Perhaps, like people, they hope for a while that it will let up or quit, but when it doesn't, finally decide, "To hell with it," and go about their regular business.

There is always considerable wildlife activity just before a heavy rain front moves in, and the duck hunter, like the fisherman, may find this short period of a half-hour or so is all he needs to fill out a limit. Once a real downpour or driving rain commences, however, all birds will usually sit tight until it lets up.

Snow

In my experience, snow is a very different story from rain. It seemingly neither helps nor hinders, and bird behavior appears the same, as it would under the same wind and temperature conditions without the snow. Many of us can fondly recall some great days of shooting during driving snowstorms, especially when hunting divers, but I've long suspected that we would have had the same shoot with the same wind, sans snow. I enjoy hunting in the snow, but the only changes I think it makes are to cut down visibility and restrict the distance a call can be heard. I doubt snow itself is much of a factor in bird movement.

The big freeze

Northern parts of the country usually have that one day each season that starts sunny and mild, but then experiences winds of gale force and a 30- to 40-degree drop in temperature. These are dangerous days that have ended the gunning career for more than one hunter caught on large, open water; but they're great for gunners on a sheltered marsh. The birds seem to sense what is about to happen and frantically seek a secure and sheltered place to ride out the night.

Bluebird days

Though goose hunters hate them, beautiful, sunshiny days are

Bright, sunshiny days usually produce the most success in timber shooting.

the mallard hunters' delight. This is the time to hunt flooded timber, potholes, and back marshes. Such days show the colors on your blocks to birds far distant, and frequently offer surprises to the hunter when ducks seemingly appear out of nowhere. The clear blue skies make birds hard to distinguish and the wise hunter keeps well down in his blind at all times. It was on such days that the springtime market hunter made some of his best wages. In bluebird weather he was constantly vigilant and he took care not to spook his game.

When in flooded timber, hunters often flail the water to create the sound of many birds feeding.

VARIETIES OF DUCK HUNTING

Flooded timber

In the early part of the century before the days of flood control and bans against spring shooting, flooded timber along our rivers and streams was thought to be the finest possible mallard hunting. It still is! No sportier type of gunning can be found than in parts of Missouri, Arkansas, Tennessee, and Louisiana, although it is not restricted to those states alone. Timber shooting is often a "walk-in" type of hunting where only boots, gun, shells, and a call are needed. It is the only type of hunting in which decoys may not improve chances of success. The hunter wades to a likely spot, leans against a tree for concealment, and calls to passing birds. In certain parts of the country it is customary to flail the water with one boot, creating ripples and a sound intended to resemble many ducks playfully at feed.

It can be a physically demanding type of hunting since bottom lands are often soft, mucky, and filled with hidden snags. Few hunters long escape an unexpected dunking, and carrying a stout stick for added support in wading is helpful, especially when there is thin or slushy ice. In such times you may wish to break

Potholes require few decoys, and these may be bunched to resemble birds at feed.

the ice and form small ponds of open water as a further induce-
ment to the birdies.

If no naturally flooded woods can be found near you, keep an
open eye for bottom timberland that could be flooded through
the use of pumps or diversion of water. The small expenditure
involved may let you obtain good shooting at less than going club
rates.

Potholes

Pothole shooting is done in woods or high grasses not necessarily flooded. A pothole is a small pond in a clearing, either natural or man-made. And if it is adjacent to a flyway or feeding
area, so much the better. Such places are attractive to most puddle ducks, and especially to mallards. Potholes may give good
hunting on stormy days when high winds make birds seek shelter,
but as with all timber shooting, they probably produce even better on sunshiny morns and afternoons.

Potholes are small—perhaps only a few yards across—but that
is all the water needed. A dozen decoys or less will work, and
the placement of them is immaterial. A good duck call, properly
used, is more important than decoys. You call not only to attract
and help the birds locate your pond, but also to assure them that
it is safe and secure for them to funnel down through the trees.

Once they have spotted your pond or decoys, circling birds
should be called rather softly. A "hard" call may bounce off trees,
giving an unnatural sound, and this can be remedied by choosing
an easy-blowing call or muffling it in your cupped hands. Shooting under these conditions can be as difficult or as easy as your
gun-pointing skill indicates. It's a tricky proposition taking birds
circling through the treetops, but a beginner's delight to wait
them out until they're dropping in on cupped wings and outstretched legs. Even in this day of crowded, privately owned, and
expensive-to-lease land, there are many of these small ponds
throughout the country that may be shot for the asking or a small
seasonal rental.

Jumping

Jump shooting is exactly what the name implies. It is a moving
type of hunting, by boat or on foot, in which you "jump" or flush

sitting birds. Small streams with many curves and bends are ideal when you are using a boat. You quietly pole, paddle, or drift with the current and hope your stealthy approach will put you within shooting distance before the ducks take alarm.

Jumping calls for quick and decisive shooting, as many birds will be nearly out of range when rising. Long shots are the standard when you are walking on ground covered by dry leaves or heavy brush that must be noisily parted for passage. Flushing birds within range when wading in marsh grass or weeds is extremely hard, unless there is a high wind to cover the sound of your approach and you are wading directly into it.

When two or more men are working a marsh, it is a good idea for one to circle the area and station himself ahead, where ducks that are jumped will fly over him. This works especially well if there is open water on either side, for birds will invariably head for it.

Walking up or jump-shooting ducks in terrain like this is fun, but it takes quick, decisive shooting and a good retriever.

Field shooting

Duck hunting in dry fields, whether of corn, wheat, or other grains, is mostly for those who are very patient, and satisfied with spotty results. Yet at times it can provide great shooting. The greatest activity can be expected during the regular feeding flights of the morning or late afternoon. The hunter hides himself in shallow depressions in the field and covers himself with a camo net, or rigs a makeshift blind from cornstalks and brush.

Field shooting is done with or without decoys, in the hope that a feeding flight will select your field as a place to dine. Once they do, it can be a nerve-racking wait while as many as several hundred birds decide whether or not to come down. They may circle time and again, leave, and then return to continue circling. Most of us can stand only so much of this before deciding to take them, even if they are not truly within range. This most often signals the end of the hunt.

Though many hunters think of Arkansas mostly in terms of timber shooting, much of its best duck hunting is provided by flooded rice paddies like these.

Both ducks and geese will often feed in a particular field for several days running if not disturbed. So the field hunter does a lot of scouting, sometimes following flights by car to establish their whereabouts. Once found, they are left strictly alone and permission is obtained to hunt that field next day. The field is entered well before daybreak and everything put in order— decoys out and hunters covered. If shallow pits are dug, fresh dirt must be removed or thoroughly scattered and the surrounding area put into as natural-appearing a condition as possible. After that, all you have to do is wait.

The late season with its bitter cold and snowy ground offers the best field shooting. When the thermometer hovers around zero and all ponds are frozen, ducks need a continuous and plentiful supply of food, and often work fields throughout the day. When there is snow on the ground, you must wear white

Duck hunting on ice can be marvelous sport, but you've got to be dressed for it.

coveralls or use a white sheet to cover you while lying between corn rows. When it is very cold, mallards will sometimes start at one end of a field and quickly feed through it, using both feet and wings to speed along. Wait until they are very close before you attempt to get into a shooting position. (This takes longer than you think, when you're bundled in bulky clothing.)

Shooting after freeze-up

The best places to hunt after a big freeze are on natural spring holes or fast-running creeks that remain unfrozen. Some clubs use pumps or aerators to keep open water, but for most of us, we must either find or create it.

Busting ice is hard work, and only sometimes worth the effort. A good-sized hole must be opened and all floating ice cakes removed. This takes time, and in severe weather a film of ice reforms almost immediately. For this reason, it is advisable to place decoys on unbroken ice around the hole's edges. If tossed into the water they will build up large rings of ice which must be continuously chipped away or your decoys will resemble miniature icebergs more than ducks.

I've heard of hunters spreading out blue plastic sheets, or pouring common washday bluing over ice and getting ducks to mistake it for open water. It sounds interesting, but I've no firsthand experience with it.

The birds themselves will often keep water open through their movement. When kicked out but not shot at, they may be depended upon to return shortly if no other open water is nearby. Concealing yourself around these holes means using piled ice, snow, or white sheets. (The less rugged should take along a small pad of white waterproof Ensolite. This closed-cell plastic foam gives good insulation if you must sit or lie directly on the ice.)

Pass shooting

In pass shooting you station yourself under or as close as possible to a natural flight path, and take a crack at the ducks that fly by you within range. The pass shooter plays a waiting game and seldom withholds a shot at anything regarded as within reasonable distance. Thus true pass shooting is the most demanding form of duck gunnery, for most birds are taken at long yardages.

Such long ranges mean that many birds will be winged or crippled, even by the fiinest of shooters. To be absolutely sure that such birds are found and retrieved, they must be dropped where they can be walked to, chased by boat, or at least where the dog can reach them. Those attempting to kill far birds over dense cover are guilty of criminal action, for many more ducks will be hit and lost than ever recovered. In almost all cases, a good dog is a must.

Pass shooting naturally calls for full-choke guns of 10- or 12-gauge, and the heaviest loads of large-size shot. In order not to cross the thin line between good and bad sportsmanship, pass shooting calls for more judgment and experience on the part of the shooter than any other form of wildfowling.

Big water

Hunting offshore on large bodies of water calls for special skills and equipment. An outboard motor is needed and it should have enough horsepower to push against high wind, or outrun approaching storms. Small boats are out. You need seaworthy craft with plenty of free board, and carrying proper flotation gear. Should disaster strike, stay with the boat, even if overturned. No matter how good a swimmer a man is, his life expectancy is a matter of minutes when he's in icy water.

If diving ducks are present they can be successfully decoyed to even the crudest of blinds or sparsely camouflaged boats. But big water calls for big spreads, and the most successful hunters number their blocks in the hundreds. Decoy anchors must be heavy and of the right shape to grasp and firmly hold the bottom or much time and energy will be spent in chasing drifting decoys.

Dead or crippled birds must be quickly retrieved since most bluebill and canvasback shooting is generally done during foul weather when seas run high.

Such shooting is for the hardy and waterwise veteran. The inexperienced should not attempt it on their own.

Over the blocks

The most "normal" type of duck hunting is from a blind with the use of decoys. While there are many variations, the idea is to entice birds to attempt to land among what they believe to be live ducks and to do so within the range of your shotgun. It is the most important and widely used method of hunting, and to avoid redundancy, it is mentioned here only in passing, as most of the rest of the book deals primarily with it.

VARIETIES OF GOOSE HUNTING

Game biologists are quick to point out that geese are not just "big ducks." The behavior of the giant birds is quite different from that of their smaller cousins, and these behavior patterns necessitate a different hunting approach. For one thing, geese are much more manageable and quicker to adapt to man's ways. Because they are now being managed by man and seemingly cooperating with him in their management, they are gaining in numbers and losing in stature. Even so, the Canada goose remains our number-one wildfowl trophy.

Long known for his wariness, the Canada was to most hunters, in most places, mostly a target of opportunity. This started changing in 1927 with the establishment of the Horseshoe Lake Refuge near Cairo, Illinois. Since that time many other refuges have been built and goose hunting around their perimeters is permitted. It's an entirely different type of goose hunting on an entirely different type of bird than our forefathers knew and hunted. Nonetheless, the Canada carries the most magical aura of all geese, and more hunters have bagged a deer than a Canada. Along with the turkey, he has often been a candidate for our national bird. To the bird watcher and asphalt ecologist he epitomizes all that is wild and free, and his romantic air is perpetuated by his monogamous devotion in mating for life. The fact that he is often as adept as humans at desertion, adultery, and divorce sullies not his public image.

For reasons not yet fully explained, the Canada goose loses much of his inherent wariness after taking residence in the refuges. This was apparent from the beginning, and in the early days, shooting geese around a refuge was more of a slaughter than a sport. This is no longer the case, to my knowledge, anywhere in the country. Whether state or federal, the refuge is managed today in the best possible way to assure good hunting

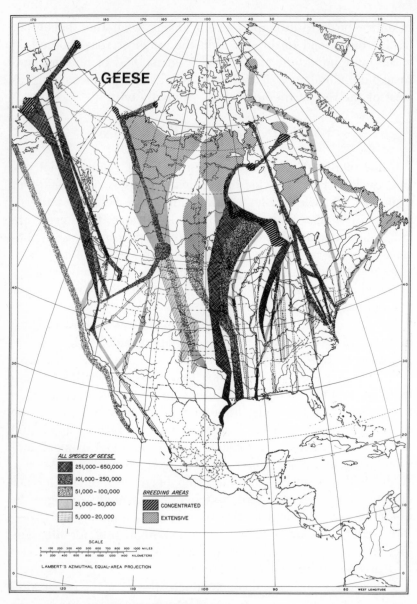

GEESE

ALL SPECIES OF GEESE

251,000 – 650,000

101,000 – 250,000

51,000 – 100,000

21,000 – 50,000

5,000 – 20,000

BREEDING AREAS

CONCENTRATED

EXTENSIVE

SCALE

0 100 200 300 400 500 600 700 800 900 1000 MILES

0 200 400 600 800 1000 1200 1400 KILOMETERS

LAMBERT'S AZIMUTHAL EQUAL-AREA PROJECTION

WEST LONGITUDE

GOOSE MIGRATION CORRIDORS

When grazing, geese usually prefer the centers of large open fields. This scene looks like Texas, but actually it's in back of the author's duck club in central Illinois.

within the controlled limits of good game management. Those about to hunt "managed" geese, please turn to Chapter 12, "Hunting the Public Areas." We are concerned here with geese in the wild.

Field shooting

Geese are grazers that spend a good deal of their time gleaning the fields. They usually choose fields that are quite large in acreage, rather isolated from outbuildings, and flat in terrain. The crops will have been either knocked down or plowed under, or they will pick fields of low grass and legumes. But exactly which field they will pick and at what time is not in the hunter's realm of knowledge.

Fortunately, geese do have a habit of working a field over until it is no longer productive for them. This might take several days and therefore often leads to their downfall at the hands of observant hunters.

When a large flock of geese is noticed feeding a field, leave them strictly alone while you try to obtain permission from the landowner. Then come back before sunrise and either dig pits or otherwise camouflage yourself in the heart of the area in which the flock has been feeding. Any pits will no doubt be of a temporary nature and need not be deep—simply enough to permit the hunters to lie down, cover themselves with vegetation, and still be fairly flush with the surrounding level of ground. The dirt dug from these pits must be carted away or covered by camouflage. No freshly dug bare earth should be visible around your pit.

In this type of shooting it may or may not be advisable to use decoys. The aim is to have everything in the area look exactly the same as it did the day before. However, this may mean a long wait. Canada geese are often late risers and may not leave

Cornfielding for Canadas can be a chancy affair, unless advance preparations are made to use "working" fields.

their overnight resting area until around eight o'clock in the morning. Since this is something you don't know for sure, you're there at sunrise. If they haven't appeared by noon, the odds are great they will not do so until an hour or two before dusk—if at all.

The behavior of Canadas depends a great deal on the weather and time of season. Snowy, blustery days with temperatures in the 20s or 30s may find them working at any time between dawn and nightfall. Let the temperature drop another 10 degrees and they may sulk all day where they are.

When there is snow on the fields, pits may be even more shallow, or dispensed with, provided the hunters are wearing white coveralls or are concealed beneath old sheets. In this latter case, make sure the corners of the sheets are pegged down so they won't flap in the breeze, and then scatter a small amount of dirt, cornstalks, or other vegetation over the sheet.

Remember, geese will seldom alight near a fence. Almost always they will pick a landing spot in mid-field, even though they may eventually feed their way to fence lines. If for some reason you cannot obtain permission to shoot a certain field where geese are working, try for one next to it. However, you will seldom get shooting here unless you use a ruse that may or may not give results and that calls for more than one hunter.

Being cleverly concealed in the adjoining field, let the geese alight and commence feeding. Then have a member of your party go around to the other side of the flock. He then walks slowly or drives a vehicle toward them and you until they become uneasy and take flight. If the part of the field they are using is not too far, and they do not become unduly alarmed or panicky by fast, noisy movement of the man or vehicle, it is quite possible that they will take off and fly over you within range.

Stalking

In stalking field geese, always crawl *downwind*. Crawl as slowly and quietly as possible, taking advantage of every natural bit of cover, and get as close to the birds as possible until you see their heads come up in alarm. When the flock is uneasy and about to take flight, you rise to your feet and run toward them, gaining as much ground as possible. Since the geese will take off against the wind, they will have to head directly toward you for a few yards before they gain flying speed and can turn away. Between your running toward them and their flying toward you, it is possible to gain 20 or 30 yards advantage.

The white spread

Another form of field shooting is known as the "white spread." This is most prevalent in the Southern wintering areas of the snows, blues, and white-fronted geese. It is done by the hunters wearing white camouflage and spreading about them as "decoys" up to a hundred or more diapers, newspapers, or white rags. The hunters then remain motionless and call to passing geese, hoping they will mistake the white rags and white-clad hunters for feeding snow geese.

The "white spread" of sheets, diapers, or even newspapers, is much used throughout the Southwest and proves highly effective on snow geese. It might be just as practical in other areas the snow geese frequent, too.

This is the traditional way of hunting geese in much of Texas, Louisiana, and our Southwestern states, but, while widely known, it seems little practiced in other areas. Since it is a proved and effective method of hunting geese in the areas it is used, I strongly suspect it would also be found productive on these species elsewhere, if given a try.

The permanent pit

Another form of field shooting is the permanent set-up. Pits are dug deeply and often are elaborately furnished, with cushioned seats, heaters, and other items of creature comfort. These pits are usually made with ladders or stairs and covered flush with the ground by sliding or parting roofs. The roof may be of steel, wood, woven grasses, cornstalks, or whatever vegetation naturally

Southern Illinois still ranks among the best areas in the country for Canada geese. It makes hundreds of pits like this one available on a daily rental basis.

This photo was taken along the Missouri River, some eighty miles north of Omaha, an area that is rapidly becoming a hot spot for snows and blues.

grows around the pit. If there is no natural pond or lake in the field, it is sometimes flooded, and then decoys are a must. While these fields are invariably chosen for their position under or adjacent to a natural flyway, they depend upon decoys—the more the better—for good shooting.

Whether your decoys are full-bodied or silhouette, you need a minimum of fifty, with two hundred or more guaranteeing better results. As geese are seen, they are called and worked as cleverly as possible to your decoys. Geese coming down from the North and new to the area may readily decoy. Suspicious flocks that have recently been shot at or are quite familiar with the area may circle time and again and show willingness to work down, but their natural cautiousness may keep them out of range for fifteen or twenty minutes. Perhaps one or two birds may break off from the main flock and come within range, sometimes even alighting among the decoys. It is here the hunters must judge whether to take the birds in hand or gamble on eventually luring the entire flock within range.

The sandbars

The sandbars formed in the center of wider rivers furnish a

traditional type of goose shooting. Birds seek these bare and isolated bars for rest and protection, as well as to drink and obtain gravel after feeding the fields. Whenever birds are seen here, they should not be flushed, but left alone to leave the bar voluntarily. When gone, the hunters can then land and conceal themselves.

Quite often there is driftwood that may be used for a sparse but effective blind. Some hunters dig shallow pits and others take along a tarpaulin throw or camouflage netting, concealing themselves under the cloth and perhaps kicking sand over it. If a boat must be used to reach the bar, it must, of course, be taken away by a member of the party.

Some go so far as to carve and use one or two seagull or heron "confidence" decoys. They swear by the effectiveness of these decoys in relieving any apprehension whatever in the returning flock.

Water shooting

Geese will return year after year to the same body of water for rest and feed. In fact, these bodies are often called "Goose Bay" or "Goose Pond," having been so named a great many years ago because of use by geese. As long as these waters remain isolated without much water traffic, they will continue to appeal to the birds in spite of the amount of hunting done on their perimeter. However, a few motorboat chases after the flock by hunters trying to take them illegally or by nonhunters for the "sport" of it will probably clear the area of birds for that season.

Some of this chasing has been done in the old belief that geese found resting on the water after long migrations may be too tired and weak to take flight for a half-hour or so after setting down. This is a doubtful story, and I have never been able to verify it. It's true, however, that geese tired from long migrating flights may sometimes alight on open water out of range, and be so reluctant to move that a boat working slowly at a distance, never heading directly toward them but tacking slowly closer all the time, will drive them toward the shore and waiting hunters. The boatman watches them carefully for signs of restlessness and soon learns to back off for a short while if they indicate that they are about to take off.

Decoying geese in open water is a far different and more difficult feat than decoying them into fields or ponds. If they do decide to light, they will invariably do so a distance from shore or blind and out of gun range. It is for this reason that most decoyed geese on big water are taken by pass shooting, or on their first swing or two of the decoys.

But there are exceptions. Low ceilings and foggy days seem to affect the birds' judgment, and a good caller can often work a large flock into his blocks without the least hesitation on their part.

7·
Blinds

Since most wildfowl have excellent eyesight, it follows that blinds play a very important role in most forms of wildfowling. For a blind is a place of concealment—a place from which to hide and shoot. A blind can take on many forms: it might be a tree platform in Arkansas, a dug-out pit in the Dakotas, a pile of rocks on the Atlantic Coast, tule weeds in California, driftwood off Southern shores, or cornstalks in the Midwest. It may be as simple as sitting inconspicuously still on a muskrat house, or as complicated as camouflaging a complete houseboat. Your blind can be a sunken barrel on a point of land, or a two-room house on stilts. It is *anything* that conceals man from the eyes of a bird, including the specialized duck boats discussed in the next chapter.

While the commonest blind-building materials are improvised from local vegetation or indigenous objects, this is not always the case, and it seems to make little difference to the birds. I find it inconceivable that a duck does not mistrust those "sore thumb" monstrosities stuck out in open water, sometimes on stilts, and made of everything from tarpaper shingles to concrete blocks. But the boys using these blinds do quite well, and having shot from them myself I can verify the fact that ducks have no hesitation coming in to decoys that surround them.

As with most aspects of duck hunting, the permissible position and construction of a blind are often limited by law. The law varies with federal, state, and local provisions, so you must be sure to check on the legality of floating or movable blinds, as well as their position, height, size, and any permit or license required in the particular area you plan to hunt.

FRAME CONSTRUCTION

With only a few exceptions (which will be noted later) the blind starts with a framework. No blueprints need be followed and your knowledge of carpentry, or lack of it, matters little.

An ideal blind: a completely natural, well-concealed "hide" for shooters that proposes an inviting landing area for ducks that is within comfortable shooting range.

Whether on land or water, the framework starts with four posts driven or placed to determine the size of the blind and furnish a foundation on which to build. When driving branches, put a flat board on top of them to prevent their splitting. The posts are joined by crossmembers, nailed, wired, or otherwise secured. Braces are added to support a floor and the framework covered in some way that will conceal the hunter.

The corner support posts can be anything sturdy at hand, from old pipe or 2x4s to small tree trunks and limbs. Smaller stuff is used for cross-bracing. Apparently there is no longer such a thing as "scrap" lumber, so you're on your own in procurement.

The floor or platform can sometimes be found ready-made by

Water blinds are harder to conceal, and often have a "sore-thumb" appearance. Fortunately, most birds aren't fussy about working to the decoys that surround them.

In certain parts of the country the hunters like their blinds big! This "duplex" is on skids so that it can be hauled from field to field by tractor.

using old doors or thick plywood, but the floor should be solid and completely covered. Don't try to get by with spaced boards. They are not only dangerous footing, but if there is room between them for anything to drop in the drink, it will.

Dimensions are flexible but should be long enough for the two, three, or four men you intend to accommodate, and the wise blind builder will add space for one more. The framework should be only high enough to reach the armpits of the shortest shooter.

If you are close to another blind, a dwelling, or anything else that shouldn't be shot at, erect a tall pole to restrict your gun swing in that direction. Depending on your shooting buddies' habits, it may be advisable to erect a gun-stop between each shooting stall, thereby preventing their shooting over each other's

Boats are often camouflaged into blinds through the use of fish netting, burlap strips and natural vegetation.

heads. Then daub mud on all freshly cut branch ends or white lumber and you have your framework.

For cold-weather hunting, windproof the inside of the blind with old carpet, gunnysacks, boards, or anything handy. The top of your framework should contain either V-shaped notches cut in the board or good-sized spikes to hold and support your gun barrel. Nothing is quite as unnerving as guns falling in the blind, and every precaution should be made to see that they don't.

BOAT BLINDS

A framed boat or water blind is constructed in the same manner with the four corner posts driven well into the lake bottom,

A separate blind or platform for the dog sounds like an extra frill, but it can sure hold down the mess and confusion inside the blind.

allowing for rise and fall of the water level. Make sure that the framework is set wide enough to accommodate the largest boat you'll use, and long enough to take boat as well as tipped motor.

If the water level is constant, the blind can be constructed with a raised platform floor so that the boat can be pushed underneath. This makes for steadier shooting than a rocking boat. Another way is to build a sloping annex at the back of the blind to house the boat. As far as I'm concerned, the dog can shake himself where he wishes, and sleep atop the lunch sack, but some hunters even build a separate platform and supporting framework for their retriever. If he'll stay there, it's less messy than pulling him in with you after each retrieve. If your blind is built high off the water, a sloping runway the dog can climb will save a lot of hunter energy.

If you intend to shoot from the boat itself, solidly nail two or more large branches or 2x4s about 8 inches apart and an inch or so under water at the end of the blind. You can then pull the bow of the boat onto this platform, which helps steady it.

ROOFING

In some cases you'll find it necessary to roof your blind to prevent discovery by circling birds, and this is especially true in mallard shooting. Try to imagine yourself in a low-flying airplane and visualize what you would see when over your blind.

Roofing can be done in several ways, perhaps the easiest and most convenient being a half top supported by the back frame of the blind, high enough to allow you to sit or stand, and offering enough cover when you pull back into its shadow. The half roof gives enough room to step forward and still shoot directly overhead. Another choice is to build a light framework, perhaps hinged with hog wire, which will hold brush or camouflage material yet be light enough to flip back as you're ready to shoot.

BRUSHING THE FRAMEWORK

Your blind is best camouflaged by whatever leaves or brush are naturally present and easily obtainable, but be sure to cut all materials well away from the blind site, and while you're at it, gather an extra supply for patching later in the season. In many cases your brush will be willow branches and, if so, they must be cut before the first freeze if they are to keep their leaves throughout the season. Oak branches are ideal in this respect, for if cut while in leaf, they can take rough handling without shedding.

Other suitable material includes cornstalks, flag, buck brush, evergreen, tule weeds, and whatever else your imagination and area can offer. A thorough job of grassing can be done by weaving grass through rolls of chicken wire. This is often so effective and long-lasting that you can roll it up after the season and use it again and again. Natural-colored snow fence held together by wire can also be rolled up and used indefinitely.

These boat blinds are being towed into the shooting area on the Mississippi.

A fine set-up: a sunken metal blind, complete with rolling top, in an Arkansas rice field.

If the entrance to your blind is exposed, you might want to try a hog-wire-hinged framework door, but usually a gunnysack or carpet drop is handier and takes more abuse. On a more permanent blind you can cobble together a plank door, drill a peephole, and nail it with brush. On water blinds subject to freezing, remember to keep all brushing material well above the water or the weight of ice build-up will strip you bare.

BRUSHING A BOAT

Old wooden boats with double gunwales provided a perfect space to fit cattails and willow sprigs, but modern aluminum hulls leave little to work with. Here again, rolls of chicken wire, well-grassed, can be attached to bolted support posts made from wood or aluminum. I've seen people run camouflage netting around the support poles, but my experience with it in rain and high winds has not been good. Those fortunate enough to have a partly covered duck boat simply camouflage it according to season by putting branches or snow on the decks. If you intend to camouflage your skiff only by painting, see the next chapter.

PERMANENT BLINDS

Those who own or have leased land for some length of time

Pretty plush! This underground pit, made from a storage tank, is comfortably heated.

In areas of heavy hunting pressure, excellent concealment is required. This brush blind was good enough to fool these mallards.

are justified in going all out in blind construction. I've shot in everything from piled-rock and poured-concrete pillboxes to welded steel tanks with sliding covers that afforded all the niceties of a good hotel. Next we'll probably see split-level condominiums.

One Nebraska goose pit I recall was made from a large underground storage tank with a cut-out top. Seats were welded onto the sides, an access stairway built, and complete kitchen facilities installed. It had one fault—your goose call sounded as if it were coming from the Carlsbad Caverns. This drawback to a steel tank can be eliminated by lining the walls with discarded carpet, the thicker the better. I much prefer steel to cement, which always seems damp and musty. To be livable, all sunken blinds must have proper drainage, which can be a problem when the blind is placed below water level.

I might mention here that when constructing a pit blind of

Propane heaters and a charcoal grill are not the least of the creature comforts some blinds afford—this one offers padded bunks as well!

An old white sheet can provide all the concealment you need on snow or ice.

any type, even a temporary one, you must carry away all dirt. In addition, if the blind is permanent, be careful not to use the same path to it every day or the worn and trampled path will act like a warning flag.

ICE AND SNOW BLINDS

While you'll find it difficult to entice most species of ducks to fly low over ice, almost all will naturally follow an icy shoreline. On the shores of large rivers and lakes, the wind-piled ice floes

offer good concealment. If the hunter wears white coveralls, or
hides under a draped sheet, he is practically invisible. A white
sheet can also be tossed over you when you are hunting snow-
covered fields or ice, and soft snow can be pushed up around you
or compacted into blocks the way an Eskimo builds an igloo.

*For pass shooting against a snowy background, a white parka makes perfect
camouflage. Now all this hunter has to worry about is selecting one bird
to aim at.*

FLOATING BLINDS

Large bodies of water, such as tidal flats or big lakes, require a different blind location daily for best results, and consequently use of a floating blind. Such blinds are usually built around a platform and floated on barrels. Some are made to conceal a boat while others are towed into place by a keeper boat which then sits off at a distance to act as retriever. This same type of blind and platform may be put on skids and sledded out on ice by hand, or pulled into rice paddies by a tractor.

A unique floating tub blind, framed in chicken wire for easy brushing.

Sunken blinds made from culvert pipe are larger in circumference, and thus roomier and more comfortable than the usual sunken barrel.

For convenience of easy portability, it's hard to beat grass-thatched chicken or hog wire, which can be rolled up to carry and quickly erected for use.

MISCELLANEOUS BLINDS

In some areas it is common practice to sink large barrels or culvert pipe on a point of land jutting into the water. As with all sunken blinds, these usually call for some form of drainage or bailing facilities. However, if you can sink culvert pipe deeply enough, a foot of pea gravel on the bottom will usually take care of any sump.

My experience with tree blinds has been quite limited, although

The last word in portable blinds is this product of Wildfowlers, Inc., which is worn on a shoulder harness. It comes in your choice of covering—brown or green camouflage, white or gray.

I can imagine occasions on which they could offer superb shooting. In my opinion, the best of all blinds for both boat and man is pushing into tule or flag where such grass grows tall in shallow water. The grass covers you completely except from overhead and it can even be bent to do that.

TOOLS

Few special tools are needed to build a rough blind, but a machete or corn knife for cutting brush, a Swedish bow saw which goes through green timber like soft butter, large spikes, binder twine as well as wire for attaching crossmembers and brush to your blind, and a sledge hammer for driving corner posts are always handy.

BLIND PLACEMENT

No matter what type of blind you build, always situate it so

Gather your blind material away from the area in which you intend to build, or you'll spell out a warning to ducks that something is wrong.

that it can take advantage of natural growth, prevailing winds, and background. Most importantly, it must be on or adjacent to a natural flyway, or a resting or feeding area. These considerations tell you the type of blind you *can* build. Other choices being equal, face your blind away from the early-rising sun. You won't have to look into it, but incoming birds will. However, weigh this against the fact that most winds come from a westerly direction and will be in your face.

In wintering areas, always build your blind before the birds arrive so they will regard it as a natural part of the landscape. But this is not so important a consideration in areas in which new birds are continually passing through.

When all is said and done, blinds are important in function, but no big deal either to design or to construct. Take a look around your own shooting area and you'll find a dozen new ideas to experiment with, and there's no reason not to use a little of your own imagination.

8·
Duck Boats

In boats, as in so many other things that have to do with
duck hunting, there is a very wide range of regional
variation and personal choice. In the golden days of duck hunting, factory-made boats were practically unknown. Duck boats
were handmade in different localities by local boatwrights, and
various different designs were developed for use in every major
wildfowl area of the country.

Many were highly specialized for a particular type of water
and the vegetation found in or around it. Such boats were
designed for safe and easy handling in shallow or deep water,
icy water, or atop ice. Boat designs became so specialized that
a hunter might own three or four different boats from which he
could choose the one that best fitted his day's hunt.

Some were for the high winds and waves of open-water canvasback shooting, others drew only a few inches of draft and were
needle-bowed to part weeds and be easily camouflaged.

Each design was usually named after its use, its maker, or the
locality in which it was most found. Many of these names are
still familiar, even though the boats no longer exist in any num-

ber. One of the most famous was the Barnegat sneak boat, but there were many other distinctive designs such as Senachwine iron skiff, Hennepin duck boat, Monitor marsh boat, Mississippi scull boat, and the Koshkonong flat boat.

Many of them are admirably designed for modern-day use, but do not have enough popularity to interest manufacturers in setting up production lines for such small numbers. While there are still a few independent makers producing true duck-boat types, their number is few and the duck hunter of today must, in most cases, be content with more general-purpose craft.

Those about to choose their first duck boat would be well advised to examine the local boats in use. As in all of duck hunting, it is usually a safe bet to follow local custom when choosing equipment, and nowhere does this rule apply more firmly than in the choice of a hunting boat. There are always good reasons for the type and design of boat found most prominently in any area, and it is the old story of "When in Rome, do as the Romans." Most likely, decades of trial and error will have dictated a design of hull that can cope with local waters and weather with safety and comfort.

A classic, low-profile duck boat makes for easy handling in shallow waters.

This wooden double-bow was made for use in the shallow but tall-weeded waters of the Duck Island Gun Club near Banner, Illinois. The members generally propel it with a push pole instead of oars.

Though it is still sometimes possible to find a wooden boat, most likely you'll take one of fiberglass or aluminum. The only rule is to buy one slightly larger than you think you'll need, and for good measure tack on another foot of length.

Fiberglass is usually (but not always) heavier than aluminum, but is less noisy to move about. It makes a better deep-water hull. For shallow water, lightweight aluminum boats are preferred. The smaller ones can be rowed across almost pure mud, and often must be. Don't forget, though, that aluminum is a natural abrasive that will chew the bluing and finish off any gun resting against it, especially if there is help from motor vibration.

PAINT

Whatever pleasure-craft type of boat you buy, it will probably be the wrong color, and if it's made from aluminum it may even retain its naturally bright and shiny finish. A couple of paint firms market a "duck-boat paint" which can be used on aluminum, usually on top of a zinc-type primer. Most of these finishes are of proved excellence, and leave a dull, nonreflective olive-drab finish. If this is too dark for your type of cover or background, it can be lightened.

If you want to experiment by mixing your own paint colors, stay clear of gloss or semi-gloss finishes. If you choose an oil-based paint, use turpentine rather than oil for a vehicle. Better yet, ask mixing advice from your paint store.

Camouflage painting is done by using different-colored areas or wide, wiggly stripes. But whether you prefer stripes or blotches, the camouflage effect will be improved at a distance if you out-line and separate the shades of color with a thin vermilion or dark-red line. This sounds strange, perhaps, but it is most effec-tive. Keep all camouflage color areas large. Most people make them far too small and this means that at a distance they tend to blend and give an overall color effect instead of remaining broken up into distinctive areas. You often need only to divide

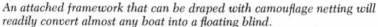

An attached framework that can be draped with camouflage netting will readily convert almost any boat into a floating blind.

the boat into three or four color sections. Small color areas of the size found on your camo clothing will prove worthless.

When thinking of a boat cover to act as a blind, don't overlook regular fishnet or minnow seine. This can be cut to fit sections of your boat, and will take rougher handling than thinner camouflage netting. Interweave the net with grasses or try tying on thinly cut canvas strips about 8 inches long, two or more net openings apart. They'll dangle down, making an excellent overhead cover for boat and occupants. The net can be propped up with sticks or poles made for the purpose and attached to the boat.

ACCESSORIES

Although most boats come without them, a set of floorboards is a great convenience. Even if your boat doesn't leak a drop, water will come into it on your boots. In addition, floorboards will let you safely put down your camera or an open box of shells. If the floorboards tend to be slippery, give them a coat of heavy paint and sprinkle it with sand before it dries.

"Runners" on the bottom of your boat convert it into a slick-sliding sled for working on ice.

When you're choosing a boat, don't just think of ease of carrying; remember all it must hold—you, your partner, dog, gun, motor and decoys.

PUSHPOLES, PADDLES, AND OARS

For short trips back and forth to the blind or to pick up the blocks, any oars will do. But if you must row any distance be sure to pick "loose" oars. The more commonly found "tight" oars have the oar pin attached to the oar itself. It is a leading cause of blisters and, just as bad, it prevents you from pulling the oars in unless you first remove them from the locks. This can be dangerous when your boat is held against a shore by high winds, and it's inconvenient around all obstructions. Loose oars are not attached, but slide through a ring of the oar lock.

Shallow water and a soft bottom mean that a pushpole, or push-paddle, is in order, and you can also use a pole for going through weeds and stumpy water or flooded timber. The pole is sometimes equipped with a duckbill which slips open when pushed against the bottom but retracts when withdrawn. A pole should be 12 to 14 feet long, allowing you to push forward, hand-over-hand, without continuously withdrawing the pole each time the boat inches forward.

You can't beat a small mud scow, drawing only a few inches of water, for use in shallow marshes.

Paddles should be long. Forget that the canoeist measures his paddle length to his eyes or chin. Get a paddle as tall or taller than you are. Most of the time you'll be standing to paddle and will want to be able to reach the water without having to do deep knee bends. Select heavy, strong paddles made from ash. Pine will splinter and split under the hard use you'll give them.

All oar handles, paddles, and poles should be sanded to remove any paint or varnish on their gripping surface, for varnish means blisters with steady use.

9.
Decoys

The 90 million waterfowl of North America belong to forty-eight species. All are decoyable, and there is evidence North American hunters have been decoying them for over a thousand years.

It is said the name "decoy" comes from the Dutch words *ende* for duck and *kooi* for cage. Originally "decoy" referred to a netted framework into which wildfowl were driven or lured for capture.

But, of course, decoy means something quite different today, and has for a hundred years. George Bird Grinnell wrote in 1901 that "Although there are conditions under which decoys are not needed for wildfowl shooting, yet usually these are essential to success. The man who proposes to gun regularly must have decoys." This statement is just as true today as it was in our grandfathers' time.

Functionally, a decoy serves a single purpose—it lures the bird within the comparatively short range of the shotgun. As to what kind of decoy and how many are needed to perform this function, few hunters agree. There are two widely divergent schools of thought. On one side are many veteran hunters who believe that anything remotely resembling waterfowl will suffice, even lumps of mud and wadded newspaper. Many of these men believe, further, that pattern means little, and that blocks may be tossed out at random.

At the other extreme are gentlemen of equal ducking experience who are willing to spend large sums for "embalmed" birds or the finest handwork modern artists/craftsmen can produce in wooden facsimiles of living fowl. With this group details of feather carving count, and each decoy must be placed precisely according to weather and conditions of hunting. Somewhere between these two extremes come the rest of us, trying to make as realistic a spread of decoys as we can with the equipment at hand, without making a federal case out of it.

While the best-set-out, most-realistic-looking stool of decoys may not actually produce better results, it's certainly unlikely that they would lessen your chances under any conditions. In other words, good decoys may not help, but they sure can't hurt. And there's another angle, too. The areas in which it is customary to use only the finest in decoys tend to be those that get the most

A gag? Not at all—those who have shot from the Neumann & Bennett "Supergoose" decoy-blind claim that geese decoy readily to it.

gunning pressure. There the birds are warier, and it may take more in decoy realism to achieve success. It is usually in the seldom-shot areas where birds have plenty of feed and resting space that they will decoy to anything remotely resembling a duck.

MODERN DECOYS

It is still possible to buy crude decoys that don't much resemble a duck, but the firms producing them are rapidly disappearing or learning to make a better product. In fact, we enjoy a better selection of factory decoys today than at any time in gunning history. Through the use of modern plastics we now have decoys lighter in weight, less subject to breakage, and with appearance equaling the best handmade wooden decoys. And while plastic lacks the individual artistry and nostalgic connotations connected with hand carving, it performs its intended use quite as well and in some cases better.

Today's trend is toward the "oversize" decoy whose large size

This spread of plastic decoys was unpainted, and just a solid dark color, but there was no difference in the behavior of decoying birds to differentiate it from conventionally painted blocks.

can be seen and recognized at greater distances. They are usually more seaworthy, riding more naturally in rough water than do those of normal size. Some firms go to the extreme by making blocks four or five times life size. Reports reaching me indicate these giant blocks produce neither better nor worse results than those achieved by the more usual oversize decoys, which are roughly twice the size of the live bird. However, under many conditions, regular big blocks do seem to pull better than normal-size ones, and would be my personal preference even though I would be hard put to prove their superiority.

Plastic decoys present a confusing array of names for the average hunter, but we can simplify things by separating plastic-body decoys into two groups—solid and hollow.

The solid, expanded-plastic foam type is fairly soft of body. It shows dents and marks of abrasion with use, but is otherwise quite rugged and capable of taking hard hunting. The hollow type is lighter in weight, has a hard finish with its colors often molded in, stands abrasion, and will not dent. But when exposed to the elements it sometimes becomes brittle and will break.

Both types have their fans and it is largely a matter of individual preference. My own choice runs toward the solid, expanded plastic, as I feel they not only hold up longer, but also ride better on the water.

There are also some rubber and soft-vinyl decoys available, and those that can be inflated are especially easy to lug to remote, hard-to-get-to spots. There are, no doubt, other special uses for which they are handy, but they are not often considered a standard gunning rig where space or weight is not of primary consideration. This can also be said of the papier-mâché decoys whose main virtue lies in their low price.

Cheaper and nearly as long-lasting is the plastic decoy sold in a solid, dull gray or black finish with the idea that you can paint your own. I have shot over a stool of these in their natural, slate-gray color and saw no difference at all on the part of decoying ducks between them and regular well-painted decoys.

PAINTING

Colors are sometimes molded into today's decoys, making them long-lasting and easily maintained. Both plastic and wooden decoy paints are available by individual color and in sets according to species, should you find a little redabbing necessary.

Some with a more artistic bent prefer to paint or repaint using colors of their own mixture. Should you have inclinations along this line, a good paint store can recommend the correct type of paint, including the new acrylics, and tell you what can and cannot be mixed. The traditional oil-base paints are fine for wood but will not work successfully on plastic.

Should you be really serious about painting, you may wish to go all-out and have two differently painted sets of decoys—a dull, bland, and sullied-colored stool for early-season use, and a colorful, brightly hued set for cold-weather use.

Some hunters always prefer late-season drakes, painted in very bright colors with a definite shine or sheen to the paint. They claim this not only does not frighten the birds, but actually pulls them in from farther away because of the high visibility. They may have something here. A well-known outdoor writer once painted his decoys in barber-pole stripes as well as red, lavender, and blue polka dots, and decoyed ducks with great success.

For all of this, shine is one thing most of us try to avoid, and generally a matte, or nonreflecting, finish is rated most desirable. The least reflecting decoys I have ever used were blowtorched, cork-bodied black ducks. This material still makes an excellent decoy, but cork blocks are now scarce and high-priced.

The sheen of wood paints can be toned down by use of turpentine and other dryers. Conversely, linseed oil and other oil mediums give brilliant colors but are highly reflective. Acrylic paints seem to work well on plastic and may be bought in semi-matte finish. And, of course, commercial decoy paints have taken care of the problem at the factory. A good rubdown with a scouring-powder paste or even a handful of wet sand does much to dim the light on glossy decoys. The old-timers used to do their painting early, and then left the decoys on a rooftop to weather until the start of the season.

If you wish to obtain realistic feathering on smooth-bodied decoys, it is traditionally done by the imprint from a lightly pressed natural sponge coated with a small amount of contrasting paint. Other feather effects may be had by using a leather "comb" and certain brush techniques. To give shadowing, heads are shaded by dragging one color of wet paint into another.

Keep in mind that there are two separate and distinct painting patterns for every species—gunning and decorative. The gunning pattern for working decoys is made up of patches of color which merge together when viewed from a distance. It is an easy-to-apply pattern that requires little painting talent. The large paint areas are easy to retouch and in use have proved as efficient as the finest feathered paint job possible. "Decorative" patterns demand realism and all the artistic ability you possess. While this type of painting is mostly done on decoys used, as the name implies, as decorative or collector's pieces, some gunners find personal satisfaction in shooting over works of art. For those interested in this kind of work I highly recommend Bruce Burk's excellent book *Game Bird Carving* (Winchester Press).

RIGGING

Some form of ballast weight is needed to keep decoys upright on the water. The old wooden decoys relied on a chunk of iron or strip of lead attached to the bottom. Most of today's decoys have a weight molded in the body bottom, or are designed to maintain a head-up position without weight, but unfortunately, many weightless designs lack stability in rough water, and nothing is as annoying as watching your blocks turn belly up. You can correct this by adding additional weight to the bottom of the decoy with strips of bar solder (expensive) or even large bolts. The least desirable method of weighting is to suspend a weight from the base on a wire or cord. It makes the decoy practically impossible to turn over without righting itself, but the entanglements at pick-up time are many. The most economical bottom weights are simply well-chosen flat rocks attached with a spot of epoxy glue. Epoxy will also hold 6-inch pieces of half-inch aluminum tubing, filled with sand and squeezed closed at both ends. Some prefer to cut a wooden keel from 1-inch board to fit, and taper both ends. This may be screwed or glued on.

LINE

Decoys are rarely sold complete with rigging of line and anchor, so you must add your own. Attach the line to the decoy body with a swivel or screw eye. For choppy water it should be

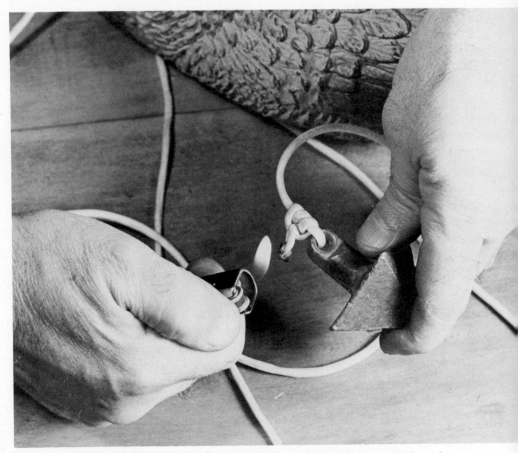

The fisherman's knot (rolling hitch) is the safest way to tie on anchors, but it's a good idea to melt a ball on the end of the rope to prevent slippage.

attached at the front underside of the decoy, but if you hunt small ponds or potholes, try tying it in the middle of your decoy. This lets the blocks swing about with the slightest wind, and gives life to your set.

Good line is no problem today, thank heavens! In the past we used cotton seine twine, sometimes tarred to prevent rotting, and boiled it in old coffee grounds for a more neutral color than its original white. Today, we buy nylon cord impervious to rotting in water, fresh or salt, and colored green, brown, or gray to match the water. Choose your color well and it will be practically invisible from the air.

Don't choose too thin a line—not because any great strength is needed, but because light line twists, kinks, and knots. Braided nylon of size 24 is much easier to handle than thinner stuff; and for use in very cold or freezing weather, even size 60 (clothesline) is preferable. Be forewarned that nylon line stretches and is slippery. Common knots like the square knot won't hold for any length of time under the constant tugging a decoy receives. However, the fisherman's knot, for use with monofilament, is easy to learn to tie and won't quit so long as you want it there. To make doubly sure, leave a ½-inch length of line at the end of the knot and hold this to a flame. This will melt the nylon and form a hard ball when it cools; even if the knot loosens, the thick and hard end of the line will prevent pulling through.

Length of line

The length of line, of course, depends on the depth of the water. As a rule of thumb, decoy line should be able to stretch to a 45° angle when the anchor is on the bottom and the decoy has reached the end of its cord. This allows the decoy to ride wave crests without lifting its anchor from the bottom.

Shallow-water gunners should measure the line to wrap exactly two or more times, depending upon depth, around the decoy body so the anchor may be either slipped over or wrapped around the decoy head. In shallow, calm waters the anchor need only touch the bottom.

Multiple lines

When there is no need to transport decoys, it may be found quicker and handier to use a multiple-line rig. This can take many forms but is basically two, six, or even a dozen decoys sharing one large anchor. To keep the individual lines from entangling, a divider bar such as a length of old water pipe is used. Decoys are tied to the pipe a foot or so apart and a small rope leading to the boat is attached to the pipe. In this way, the pipe may be pulled ashore at the end of shooting, bringing with it up

Decoy anchors come in various shapes for use on different types of bottoms: shown here (from top left) are an over-the-head knobbed anchor, a plain over-the-head (which can easily be cast with a sand mold), a pipe mold, a commercial pyramid type, a muffin-pan mold, and a pipe mold made into a grapple by hammering in spikes.

to a dozen decoys at one time. When tying to the pipe, alternate the length of line on each individual decoy so they do not look like soldiers in a row.

A convenient variation is a heavy rope or length of chain with an anchor on each end. Decoys are then tied to the rope or chain just as on a pipe. This allows a more flexible placement of the decoys, but greater care must be taken to avoid tangling.

ANCHORS

The shape and size of a decoy anchor is regulated by the type of water and bottom on which it is to be used. The commercial decoy anchors are not particularly expensive in themselves, but because their weight makes them costly to ship, most of us make our own.

Anyone who has access to scrap lead, a melting pot, and a blowtorch is in business. Molds are made and sold, but they, too, are hard to find and expensive. So it may be easier to use a bit of ingenuity and improvise a mold from such things as a muffin pan or an egg poacher. Both produce an anchor of good shape and weight for sand or mud bottoms, and the weight can be varied by the fullness of the mold. A pound and a half will handle over-size decoys in the roughest weather, and you can scale down from that.

The loop on which to tie the decoy line is usually heavy wire, set into the mold with the lead poured around it. Make the wire loops large enough to slip over the head of the decoy. Heavy-gauge aluminum wire is excellent for fresh water use.

Mushroom-shaped anchors are fine for soft bottoms, but don't hold well among rocks, so there we use the grapnel type. Since this form of anchor depends more on grabbing and holding the bottom than on its weight, it can be made from fairly light stock. Usually, there are three or more hooks and they may be soldered up from wire stock or bought commercially, and the factory product is readily available in areas where this form of anchor is needed. Of course, anchors can also be made from almost any-thing—half brickbats, pipe elbows, wagon bolts. You name it, and I'll bet it's been used.

The fishhook pattern. If all goes well, the ducks will work in at the point of the broad arrow.

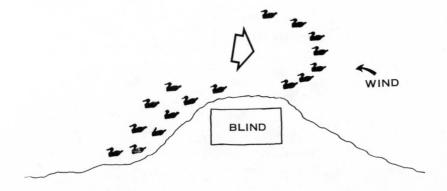

PATTERN AND PLACEMENT

Most of us simply toss decoys overboard in helter-skelter fashion, a system that sometimes seems to work as well as the most scientific placement. But the well-rounded duck hunter should certainly know decoy "patterns" whether he chooses to use them or not. Many have names such as "J," "fish hook," or "crook," all of which refer to the same pattern but have different names in different localities.

The pattern attempts to make birds fly over or near decoys or alight among them in a certain way. And since ducks usually make a final swing to land into the wind, these patterns are set in regard to wind, blind position, and surrounding terrain. There are no hard or set rules unless it would be to follow local custom.

If decoys are set in a "V" pattern and headed into the wind, in

Decoys should usually completely surround an open water blind. A landing space is left at the point of the broad arrow.

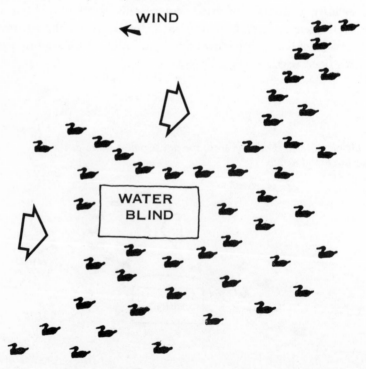

all probability decoying ducks will alight in the opening of the V. And, of course, the most desirable position for this V opening would be directly in front of your blind.

The "inverted fish hook" pattern, which is set exactly as the name implies, intends that the birds should land in the bend of the shank—and sometimes they do.

There are also "oval" patterns, with the landing space left in the center, and "Y" patterns, which are used around points of land with the blind placed on the point which enters the opening of the Y.

The "trailer" pattern features a main body of decoys bunched at random but stringing a tail of single-file decoys to whatever length is felt desirable.

The most practical instructions I've seen on decoy patterns are to be found in the late Ralf Coykendall's fine little book, *Duck Decoys and How to Rig Them* (Holt, Rinehart and Winston).

There is a difference between pattern and placement, although both are designed to accomplish the same end. It is good to remember the majority of a duck's life is dedicated to shoveling it in one end and pushing it out the other. A duck is a straight tube and *food* is the motivating force that guides most of his activities. Thus you should set your decoys with this thought in mind. Feeding ducks that are at ease and filling their bellies follow no set pattern, but are spread apart throughout the feeding area. In fact, a raft of ducks closely bunched together usually indicates nervous birds about to depart. Remember this while flinging out your blocks.

Even a small number of decoys can be made to appear more numerous when widely spread apart. The only rule here is not to set them too far from the blind. It's pretty hard to set them too close and there is nothing wrong with decoys against, around, and behind the blind.

When using a mixed stool of puddle ducks such as pintails, mallards, and black ducks, place the pintails on the outside of the spread. This is only because decoys showing a lot of white are more easily seen. By the same token, your black-duck blocks should be placed closest to shore and preferably by themselves, simply because that's the way black ducks most often act.

When using a mixed stool of goose decoys and duck decoys, the geese should be in a separate group, by themselves and upwind. For some reason, perhaps a lower pecking order, ducks don't like to light directly ahead of geese, but show no hesitancy in landing quite close behind them.

I don't like to mix puddle and diving ducks such as mallard and canvasback. When using both, it is better to set them in separate groups. For example, when hunting from a shore blind, the mallards would be closest to the blind with the diving duck

This is a nice spread of decoys and a good blind position, but the blocks are set much too far out from the blind.

Even if you're not hunting a light-colored species, a few decoys with a lot of white make effective attention getters. Notice how the drake canvasback decoy stands out from the duller hen mallard blocks.

spread farther out. Again, the large patches of white on diver-duck decoys are a good attraction, helping to bring attention to your adjacent puddle-duck spread. This set-up can be used advantageously to lead birds over a certain position. Low-flying mallards and pintails often skirt the edge of rafting diver ducks rather than flying directly over them. You can capitalize on that habit by placing a large stool of divers in such a relationship to the blind that mallards winging around them will fly directly over you. I've seen this same principle applied by parking a boat or other unnatural object at a certain spot so ducks will flare or divert their flight around it. All of which leads us into *unintentional* flaring.

If decoying ducks flare or become suspicious at a certain distance, look around you, for something's wrong. They are spotting either you, your outboard motor, or perhaps a reflection from your Thermos-bottle top. Whatever the offending object, cover it up or get rid of it.

The reason for flaring can sometimes be puzzling and might be caused by such simple things around the blind as well-worn paths, empty shell casings, or a discarded lunch wrapper. So be a good housekeeper in the vicinity of your blind.

HOW MANY DECOYS?

Having tossed your decoys out before sunrise, it's often advisable to reset your spread by light of day. The size of your spread is conditional, and not only on how many decoys you have. I once shot over a spread of 1,400 single-set decoys in an Arkansas rice field! When I asked my host if this many were really needed, he said, "Only if you like to shoot ducks."

I've noticed large spreads are not as common now as in the past. This is probably due to the relatively small bag limits of today. Few hunters think that the labor involved in setting out and picking up a couple hundred decoys is justified by a two- to four-duck daily limit.

Ducks don't seem to be fussy about relative size; these jumbo mallard decoys are actually of regular goose size, but they work fine.

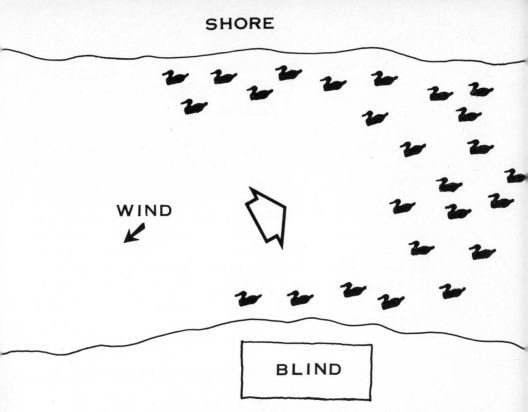

SHORE

WIND

BLIND

Sometimes decoys are used to intentionally divert ducks, and this kind of rig can do it: decoys placed directly in front of the blind invite birds to light outside of them, in a narrow strip of water such as this.

Ideally, the size of your spread should be dictated by the type of ducks and water you hunt. A small pond, or tree-lined pothole, on which you set a half-dozen decoys can produce excellent mallard shooting, while big, open water calls for a much larger stool. In my judgment, lake or large river hunting means a minimum of three dozen blocks for mallards, while twice that number is barely adequate for successful shooting of canvasbacks or bluebills, and twice again is closer to the normal successful rig. Since larger stools almost always pull better, you are limited only to the number of decoys you have and are willing to put out. If you are hunting in crowded quarters with blinds only a few hundred yards apart, you'll note that the biggest spread usually gets the most shooting.

PICKING UP

Retrieving several dozen decoys at end of day can be a problem, especially in high wind or slush ice. When water is shallow and the footing firm, it is probably best to wade. And while some find the commercial decoy "aprons" beneficial, most only take a half-dozen or so decoys per trip. I think it's easier to push a boat ahead of you and fill it with decoys as you pick them up. Even a large washtub can be utilized this way. Otherwise, the duck hunter's best friend is still the produce or gunny sack, free for the asking from your friendly grocer. They hold about a dozen blocks each and once the decoys are ashore, prevent them from frosting in the morning.

A realistic spread of mixed snows and blues, with Canadas separated in the background. These are Henriettas, by G&H Decoys.

These full-bodied field-model geese by Otter Plastics Co. have separately molded bottom sections that can be removed, leaving a flat-bottomed decoy for water use.

If the water is deep and a boat must be used, it's handy to drive a nail halfway through the end of an oar. This can be used to hook around the decoy line for easy retrieval. If it's possible to use a motor, the easiest procedure is to skirt the perimeter of your spread, picking up on the run in ever-decreasing circles.

No matter what the temperature of water or air, you'll need a large pair of waterproof rubber gloves to prevent freezing your fingers. Though it is best to wrap your blocks as they are picked up, when the water is rough I'd advise you to get them in quickly, any way you can, and sort them later on shore.

DECOY HINTS

While some hunters would never dream of mixing different-size decoys, others have excellent success in doing so. Perhaps one of

A typical East Texas "white spread" of rags, set for snow and white-fronted geese. You've never lived until you've seen birds coming in to this set-up, for you're dressed in white, too, and they're decoying to you.

the reasons is that ducks on the water have little uniformity, and there may even be a certain falseness about a man's spread consisting of decoys of all the same type from the same maker.

If you feel you need duller plumage for early-season use, try using 90 percent hens for this early shooting, leaving drakes for later use. The disadvantage is that hens considerably darken the spread, cutting visibility.

In late season when birds are in full and brilliant plumage, your decoys may have acquired a muddied and sullied hue. It might be a good idea to think about washing the lot in detergent, which usually brings out their original color.

Field mice are attracted to expanded foam. I doubt that they actually eat it, but they sure like to nibble out ugly chunks. If you store decoys in an outbuilding, be sure they are protected.

A string of large fishing-seine floats painted black with a broad white stripe is excellent to increase a diving-duck decoy spread.

Some hunters highly recommend "confidence" decoys. These can take the form of one or more seagull or crow decoys, nonchalantly perched atop the blind, or even large heron or crane silhouettes. Since these birds are quite wary, they convey to ducks the idea that nothing is amiss.

If you have a few decoys whose heads are broken or lost, try attaching a weight to the breast. This pushes them tail up/head down to make them represent "dippers" or puddle ducks at feed.

Dead ducks may also be used as decoys by propping their heads with small sticks. It works like a charm, but is somehow distasteful to me.

White plastic bleach bottles have successfully decoyed pintails, and snow geese as well.

Remember that the most realistic and best-set-out stool of de-

Ice build-up can be a problem in this kind of weather, but it helps to heavily wax the sides of your decoys.

coys will seldom pull ducks over any great distance from their normal flyways.

DECOY COLLECTING

A sudden surge in interest in decoys as a form of folk art has sent collectors prowling around beach houses and duck shacks, not to mention auction rooms. Fortunately, there are still treasures to be found. The gun collector of today doesn't harbor much hope of turning up a Colt Patterson in an attic, but the serious decoy

When there's frost around, it's a good idea to cover your decoys; otherwise you'll have to dunk each one in water to rid them of white frost as you set them.

Decoys are now considered a form of folk art, and have jumped astronom-ically in price in recent years. Here Willis Pennington examines a block from his fine collection.

These gunning-model decoys are true modern works of art. The goldeneye is Jim West's work, the hen mallard by Ken Ingraham.

168 · THE DUCK HUNTER'S HANDBOOK

fancier has a fair chance of turning up examples of the work of better-known makers. In 1934 Windward House published a book by Joel Barber called *Wild Fowl Decoys* that started it all. This is still the bible of collecting, but new and excellent works are appearing regularly. One such is George Ross Starr's *Decoys of the Atlantic Flyway* (Winchester Press).

As in all collecting, there are pitfalls for the novice. As Hal Sorenson, publisher of the *Decoy Collector's Guide,* points out, "All old decoys are not 'Rembrandts' and values can range from twenty-five cents to five hundred dollars and more." Some people have the impression that every old block is worth a mint. This simply ain't so. Much depends on whether the maker is well known, and on the condition of the decoy itself. Those that have been repainted drop rapidly in desirability. While the handmade decoy is most sought after, there is a brisk market for early factory decoys, too. These will, no doubt, appreciate in value as the handmade goodies are gobbled up.

Since the hobby is growing at a rapid rate, there is more and more interest being shown in contemporary carving. Some of the decorative decoys made today by carvers Bruce Burk, Bob Kerr, and Jim West will warm the heart and hearth of any duck hunter. There are now many decoy shows or contests held around the country and attending them is a pleasurable way to see what is happening in the field.

Many old decoys have been used for kindling, because few of us realized what their value would be in a short time. So those of you who have tossed the old man's blocks into the attic had better take another look at them. You might have a small fortune going to dry rot. The very least you can do is uncover true American folklore art that should be preserved.

10·
The Art of
Duck Calling

The first morning I was allowed to attend an opening-day breakfast, my grandfather handed me a duck call. Then, along with eggshell coffee, jowl bacon, and buckwheat cakes, came explicit instructions that I was not, under any circumstances, to blow it while in the blind.

I was young then. Since that time I've mingled with some pretty fair hoot-and-grunters such as "Dud" Faulk, Phil Olt, Chic Major, and others. They *still* give me the same advice.

But in spite of the howls I'll hear from old-timers, I claim there is better calling today than at any time in the history of waterfowling. Duck calls are better made and the instructions clearer.

For instance, my old man's primary passion in life was hunting ducks. He chased 'em, man and boy, for sixty years and was a deadly shot on high-flyers and drop-legs alike. But he was a lousy duck caller. He had one call, a sort of prolonged grunt. But then, too, his shooting cronies (an assorted group of doctors, lawyers, and bootleggers) made about the same noise. All were good and successful hunters, if not accomplished callers. They never learned to call well because they never really needed to know how. The greater part of their hunting life revolved around live decoys, feed pens, long seasons, and lots of birds.

169

Dud Faulk, famous Louisiana call maker and a world and national champion caller, says the key to calling is knowing when *as well as* how *to call.*

Those were the "good old days." Today, duck hunting is a new game with a new set of rules. A call, and knowing how to use it, can often mean the difference between roast mallard and a TV dinner.

You can learn to call ducks. Even if you don't have anyone to teach you, there are records available to at least let you hear what a call should sound like. Instruction records by Faulk, Olt, and others will, with practice, teach you enough to actually lure birds under favorable conditions.

Of course, you need know not only the sounds, but which calls to use and when to use them. That, my friend, is not a skill acquired by correspondence course. You see, calling is a regional art. They don't call ducks the same in Illinois as in Arkansas, even though they may be the same birds. A classy caller from Chesapeake Bay might easily strike out on a Dakota pothole. Even on home grounds, you don't blow the same in timber as you do on open water. And as with all good musicians, you must learn to vary tempo and tone.

Tone is odd. I've heard some calls that sound awful, but really pull 'em in. Some of those little old squeaky calls grab ducks like they were on a string. In fact, when there is a lot of calling going on around you, you'll find that a very high-pitched call will produce better results than a more normal tone.

Even with the best of calling and conditions, there are days when the birds just won't respond to any amount of pleading, and there isn't much you can do about it but wait 'em out. On the other hand, any call that makes a noise may turn the trick on those nice, sunshiny mallard-morns, or when the barometer busts its bottom on the afternoon before the big freeze.

If you are serious about learning to call, pick a few pointers from the *real* experts. Listen to the raspy quack of that old hen mallard lost in an early-morning fog, and the contented chuckle of birds at feed. Try a duck marsh on a quiet, moonlight night—it's all part of your training.

Don't overlook records made for the electronic callers. Though mostly live recordings that are illegal to use while hunting, they can be of great help in learning basic calls in your living room.

The problem today is that you seldom have enough space to properly call ducks into your decoys. You may be a caller of championship caliber, but all the caterwauling around you will nullify your most artistic efforts. You can work on birds for ten minutes and just when they decide to drop in, the guy in the next blind will choose that moment to ground-swat a mudhen and you can watch your birds claw for altitude.

How much calling to do is a much mooted question. One school of thought considers calling only an "advertisement" or attention getter—you make a few quacks at a passing duck to draw his attention to the decoys. Once this has been done, all calling is stopped. It's a theory usually founded on experience of those who have never truly mastered the duck call. Because of their lack of proficiency, it is probably the wisest course—for them.

The opposite is the guy who never stops blowing from the time he gets into the blind until he leaves. But in duck calling, as most of life, moderation seems to be the key. Between the two extremes is the hunter who has learned several different calls, but most importantly has learned to judge callable ducks. This is an art in itself and takes years of "bird" watching. The old-timer can tell at a glance whether it's really worthwhile giving a "highball" to a passing flock. He can tell "working" birds from those that have their flight plan already mapped out.

Rare is the caller who can produce any results at all from large flocks of high- and fast-flying birds. Instead, the wise caller saves his breath for the bird that is loafing along with slow-flapping wings and alternate glides.

This is a working duck, head moving to-and-fro, seeking just such a safe and sheltered area as your decoys now occupy. Often he is leery, wanting to come in, but still by instinct somewhat decoy-shy. He'll probably continue to circle until quite sure everything is safe. And this is where the expert caller can help him make up his mind, settling him down with soft burring sounds and an almost continuous feeding chuckle. Even then, never call

Two or more callers can usually outpull just one. Those with only a fair amount of talent can cover each other's mistakes, but two expert "grunters" are even better.

There are times when a good call and the knowledge of how to use it are more valuable than decoys.

when birds are directly overhead; just remain motionless and very quiet.

The greeting, or highball, is the primary call. Its purpose is to attract and interest passing birds in your decoys. It's also by far the most difficult. It is done in different ways in different areas, but retains one point in common wherever it is done successfully. No matter what the preamble, it reaches a certain note and stays there in perfect pitch without break.

There are many different calls, again depending on the locale in which you are hunting and the type of bird to be lured. Strangely enough, almost any breed of duck will respond to a good mallard call. Even big-water canvasbacks and bluebills will swing toward your blocks on a mallard call instead of their own "burrrrrrrssssss." This, of course, means the call has drawn their attention to the decoys, which are a stronger attraction than the sound of the call.

The West Coast pintail shooter is addicted to his whistle call, while the Midwestern hunter does quite well on sprig with the mallard quack. Actually, the pintail calls in both ways. There are wooden and plastic whistle calls sold, but a regular metal dog whistle with the pea removed has more volume and can be held in the mouth, leaving both hands free for the gun.

To the novice, the most mystifying aspect of calling is that good and successful calling seldom sounds like a duck. This is not to say it can't, just that many styles of calling do not, even though they produce deadly results.

Apparently, this holds true the world around. The Italians, for instance, are decidedly unsuccessful with mouth-blown calls, but quite adept at calling deep-water ducks by ratchets. The James Bay area Indian guide has no trouble pulling geese in over the flats with hoots and yelps only faintly resembling the bird's natural call; and many Mexican guides apparently shout Spanish obscenities.

SELECTING A CALL

Duck calls can be broken down into two basic types, "soft" calls and "hard" calls. Each has its functions. A hard, raspy call has great carrying power, but will often scare shy birds. (A gloved hand can be used to muffle, or soften, such a call, and some old-timers would dip their call into water for the same effect.) On the other hand, you need volume for distant ducks over big water. Other effects may be had by pointing the call at the water, against the side of the boat or blind, or perhaps into your hat. This is sometimes a help when hunting from a metal tank or pit, and prevents ringing.

Selecting your first duck call will offer no problem if you stick to any of the better-known brands in the popular price range. All are made to sound off with a minimum of huffing and puffing. The beginner will find that a $3 or $4 call answers his purpose as well as a fancy-grained twenty-bucker. Whatever call you buy for this season won't be the one you want next year. Most hunters change brands of calls as regularly as underwear.

My unofficial guess would be that the most popular duck call ever made is the hard rubber Olt. It has tremendous volume and is still one of the finest big-water calls made. But high-volume, raspy calls have a way of bouncing around for timber shooting, and for this type of work the softer Faulk calls are hard to beat.

Calls have been made from all kinds of material. The majority

In "pea-soup" weather, a call means everything. Dense fog slows duck movement almost to a halt, but flying birds can be called quite easily within sight, which means easy gun range.

of wooden calls are made from American walnut, but almost every variety of wood has been used, and even bamboo is popular in the bayou country of Louisiana.

Exotics such as rosewood and zebrawood make dense, beautiful calls of exceptional tone, especially when made in a larger size. However, they require care as they are prone to splitting once the finish is chipped or worn. Charley Perdew, of decoy fame, made splendid calls from cedar and prevented their splitting by the use of metal retaining rings. For permanency, the same would have to be done with myrtle, apple, cherry, and other woods offered in custom-made calls. I have also seen excellent calls made from bowling balls, brass or lead pipe, and as in all products of this age, plastic.

Reed material is now largely made of Mylar, but this is also a matter of taste and many prefer hard rubber, brass, or nickel silver. The very fine-sounding Yentzen call has a unique double reed giving a resonance unlike any other. No matter what the material, most of the boys scrape, sand, or otherwise rework the reed to suit their own way of calling. Some makers "age" their reeds, claiming new Mylar will take a set. Choose a reed somewhat stiffer than you prefer. It will limber with use.

All reeds stick up, or "freeze," on occasion. It's an occupational hazard of duck hunting. At times they simply clog with willow leaves, cornstalk, or bits of ham sandwich, but most often through excess moisture. This is remedied by blowing hard through the opposite end, vigorous shaking, or taking the call apart to dry. The call manufacturers wouldn't have it any other way, as this operation creates their largest replacement market.

In cold weather the call may actually freeze. If so, shove it under your armpit or blow warm breath into it until it thaws. This is one reason you often see grizzled veterans with two or more calls strung around their necks.

There is no magic shortcut to calling. The "shake 'em," or bellows-hose-type call, will give a good chatter or chuckle if you've never learned to make this sound on a regular call; but that is about the limit of its usefulness. You can learn to chuckle with your own call by saying the words "ticket-ticket-ticket" over and over, faster and faster, into your call. You'll be a bit tongue-tied at first, but it will come. While the simplest of calls, it will impress your non-calling buddies and sounds great in a tavern.

Like a musical instrument, artistry on the duck call demands proper tutoring and constant practice. But such sounds may be

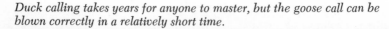

Duck calling takes years for anyone to master, but the goose call can be blown correctly in a relatively short time.

less than melodious to those around you. Unless you live "where never is heard a discouraging word," you may find it more convenient to keep your call in your automobile and practice while going about your normal business. You'll get a lot of practice, along with some funny looks.

In the beginning you may turn away more birds than you pull in. Don't let it bother you. Perfection will come and the first duck you *know* you actually called into the blocks will more than make up for past failures.

Casting such self-satisfaction aside, you'll probably find that two or more just-fair callers will outcall one good caller, and this is decidedly true on geese. I am assuming that each man knows when and when not to call, or takes his lead from someone who does. Unison calling helps cover any tonal mistakes by the individual and adds to the liveliness of the sound.

GOOSE CALLING

Fortunately, goose calling is a considerably less demanding art than duck calling, and almost anyone can become a respectable caller on the big Canadas with only a few hours of instruction and a good call. This is probably due to the fact that while a duck call is blown from the diaphragm and is actually more like grunting than blowing, the goose call is blown from the mouth, which requires much less practice.

The call should be grasped on the tone end between the web of your thumb and forefinger, the other hand then brought up to form a cup, using both hands. The opening should be straight up. By so doing, you can control the tone and volume of the call by closing or opening your fingers.

In spite of what you may have heard, the call is not made by starting on a low note and breaking into a high. The highball for Canadas is simply one note—a short, high-pitched honk most easily done by saying the word "hut" or "hoot."

You first call to passing geese by making this one "hut" and pausing five to ten seconds. Simply repeat and pause until the birds break and head toward you. Then immediately shorten and speed up the "hut" barks of the feeding call. Do not let up on this call until you are ready to shoot. As Ken Martin says, "Blow it

Charlie Sullivan, Illinois champion voice caller in action. Charlie can demonstrate that mouth calling can be superior to most manufactured goose calls.

right in their faces." And keep in mind you are trying to imitate the call of only one goose. There is no reason for you to try to sound like a flock.

Some hunters become very good at calling geese by mouth. But for even those so talented, there are drawbacks, the main one being that it's hard to call for many days straight. Another is that the range of the voice is much more limited than that of a call, and hence most hunters find that as their voice deepens with age (barring castration) the effectiveness of their calling suffers.

For sheer unpredictability, snow and blue geese take the cake. These silly damn birds usually sit and travel in large numbers, making too much noise themselves for a call to be heard. You

Specklebellies (white-fronted geese) will stool in well to a white spread, if the caller knows how to duplicate their cackling laughter.

might call to passing skeins for ten years without results; then again, perhaps the first honk you let out will find a couple hundred trying to sit in your lap. Most guides I've watched calling snows simply utter an occasional "yelp" which doesn't seem to either frighten or attract the birds.

My personal opinion is that these geese respond to calling just about as poorly as my palate responds to them. Even in the Gulf Coast wintering grounds where the lesser snows are most numerous, they are invariably smoked or barbecued before being consumed, and to my taste, the greater snows of the Atlantic Flyway are only slightly better. I'll cast my vote instead for the white-fronted goose, or "specklebelly." He decoys readily to a good caller, and he roasts up well, too.

COLLECTING CALLS

Now that decoy collecting has reached a somewhat advanced stage, many of the same collectors are turning their attention to the older duck calls—a classic example being the calls made by Charles Perdew, of Henry, Illinois. Many of his were crudely hand-carved to portray a flying mallard, and collectors offer prices in the hundreds.

Fred Allen, of Monmouth, Illinois, made many calls during the closing years of the last century and they found their way throughout the country. They, too, bring big prices. A real prize would be one of Charles Grubb's calls made in Chicago from 1893. Most are of red cedar and those with a silver collar and silver reed are much sought. And perhaps equally attractive to the collector would be the Eureka call by Charles Ditto. But many authorities claim the top collectable would be a Glodo.

At this stage, no one really has any idea how many different calls were made in the old days, so it's a wide-open field. Even calls made now or in the past few years by individuals, perhaps the last of their breed, will show increased interest in this age of mass factory production. The public library in Stuttgart, Arkansas, houses a large call collection assembled by Chick Majors, a famous call maker in his own right.

Ken Martin's goose call has never changed its easily recognized shape, so future collectors may have a problem dating early and late models. But there are a few that are highly sought even today by the collector. They were made from rosewood, before Ken found he was allergic to it.

The Faulk Custom model offered in the 1950s, made oversized and from rosewood or tigerwood, now commands well over double its original price; and I would look for the same to hold true someday shortly for his giant call that actually worked but was made more for display purposes. All calls made by Turpin and Dennison have at least tripled in value in few short years.

Call collecting can be an interesting off-season hobby for the waterfowler, just like decoy collecting.

11·
Retrievers

R etrievers are great conservationists. Under most conditions they're desirable and under some, an absolute necessity. Thus, as far as I'm concerned, there's no argument as to whether or not the wildfowler should have a dog; the only questions are "Which breed?" and "Should you keep him in the house?" and "How do you get him trained?"

Dog owners form strong opinions, which they are willing to fight about, and no matter what advice I give, I know that some will disagree with me and let me know it in no uncertain terms. Nonetheless, since I really don't care what kind of dog you have, or where you keep him, as long as you have one and train him or get him trained, perhaps I'll be forgiven for expressing the following strictly personal preferences.

KENNEL DOGS VS. FAMILY DOGS

Having hunted with both pampered pets and field-trial champions, I must admit the very finest I ever shot over were four characterless robots—kennel-bred, -raised, and -trained; their entire life directed toward one goal by a highly professional handler. I admired their work, but felt no emotion toward them. Sharing a blind with one of them was both eerie and confidence-shaking. It was as if the hunter didn't exist except as another impersonal machine whose function was to drop ducks, and who would have perhaps been bitten if he missed. I fondly recalled my old Irish water spaniel whose indifference to perfect performance more often matched my own.

I've been given to understand this is not the right attitude. Other than what I've read and observed, I have little working knowledge of correct training procedures. But being on the using rather than selling end, I have always believed a retriever is not only handy as a pocket on a shirt, but good company, too. I don't hunt nearly as well as I've been trained to do, and I continuously

As far as I'm concerned, the retriever should be considered just as essential a part of wildfowling wherewithal as the gun, shells or duck calls.

make damnfool mistakes, so I can forgive my old buddy for much the same action. If he's likable and has a good character, he's got it made. After all, he's primarily a friend ten months of the year, and a working dog for only two.

WILDFOWLING DOGS

Many of us tend to self-train dogs and expect too much for the effort given. However, it is a personal choice having to do with each man's temperament, attitude, and way of hunting, if not daily life itself; and whatever your life-style, there is a breed of retriever whose ways most match your own.

Top dog among America's duck and goose hunters, the black Lab displays a level of performance that justifies his popularity.

Black Lab

Even to the nonhunting public the name "black Labrador" means "retriever," and such fame is deserved. His qualifications for the job are impressive—he's a strong swimmer, can take cold water, has a fine nose, and is persistent in searching out cripples. He is one of the easiest dogs to train, and he often does a fine job instinctively. Being even-tempered, gregarious, and affectionate, he makes a great off-season companion whose manners and lack of body odor make him house-welcome even to the ladies.

Chesapeake

For the no-nonsense type of guy taking his hunting seriously, the Chesapeake is admirably suited. He'll outswim, outweather, and outfight any other breed of dog on the marsh. He will belong and be loyal to you and you alone, showing great (if somewhat

The yellow lab has many fans who believe his neutral coloring blends better with duck-marsh vegetation than darker hues.

The Chesapeake Bay retriever is a solid professional—the kind of fetch dog that performs well under the toughest conditions.

rare) affection in his own way, provided no one else is watching. He has a low tolerance toward fools, children, and amateurs. He's the biggest, roughest, toughest professional in his line of work.

Golden retriever

The golden has a lot of class. He's a big, handsome dog with all the brains and brawn needed for a top-rate job of retrieving under all conditions. Professionals tell me they have never handled a dog quicker to learn or easier to train. He's also a nice guy—protective of his own and a fine companion, but perhaps a bit large and overly active for more refined households.

While the Lab is more popular, recent years have found the golden gaining acceptance and recognition. Those wanting a good-natured, capable performer should become acquainted with the golden before making their final choice.

Irish water spaniel

A real clown on off-hours but serious about his work, the Irish "rattail" water spaniel is great just to be around. Occasionally his actions match his mood, which may irk those owners demanding a constant level of performance. His nose knows and he's an excellent as well as enthusiastic swimmer, but can't take cold water to quite the extent of a Lab or Chesapeake. His naturally oily coat

Golden retrievers tend to be "one-man" dogs, but with their good looks, great swimming ability and high intelligence, they are rapidly increasing in popularity.

can also get a bit rancid-smelling around the house, which lessens his popularity as a family pet, but all in all, he's a dog with all the wit and charm anyone could ask of a hunting partner.

American water spaniel

Smaller and perhaps less enthusiastic than the Irish, the American water spaniel is also less subject to moodiness and insistence on doing things his way, and so is more easily trained. He's a friendly fellow who wants to please and usually does. With his spaniel nose, he is one of the best in seeking out cripples in heavy cover. Like the Irish, he's a good swimmer but can't take icy water or really rough going as well as the larger, heavier-coated dogs.

TRAINING

Whether to buy a trained retriever, have your present pup professionally trained, or do it yourself is a decision only you can make. It depends on your economic position as well as the degree of proficiency you expect from the end result.

Professional training costs money, and I'm convinced it is better not starting at all unless you are willing to pay for leaving the dog with the trainer the length of time he feels is needed to turn out a finished performer. Many intend letting the trainer do the early work with the owner smoothing out the rough spots at leisure. This usually gives worse long-term results than no professional training at all.

Almost anyone with common sense, time, patience, and some rudimentary knowledge of training can do a good enough job to please himself. Even those not easily pleased are more apt to accept or overlook faults in their dog if they result from their own methods of training. However, any training takes time and intelligent application. There are no shortcuts to success, and the ill-informed self-trainer who tries to shorten the process by overuse of modern electrical devices may find his Fido is becoming more vegetable than dog.

The old adage "You gotta be smarter than the dog" still holds true. To train a dog requires a certain amount of study and

To avoid losing ducks on water like this, the gunner and his well-trained dog work as partners—though the gunner may consider himself only a junior partner since he has little to do but give signals.

preparation. You should read not one book, but several on the subject, as few authors agree on any method or way of training. You should have several viewpoints from which to choose the course most logical and likely for you to follow.

Some training and discipline is a must, if only to insure that you are welcome hunting with others. An out-of-control, wildly running dog will get you blackballed from more hunts than a tendency to tremble violently every time you handle a gun.

12·
Hunting the Public Areas

Though many are unaware of the fact, the would-be duck hunter in many areas can become a "member" of a millionaire's duck club for an outlay ranging from nothing to $25 per day. These "clubs" are private, state, and federal shooting areas. Your "membership" may be obtained by reservation, drawing, or personal appearance on a first-come, first-served basis, depending upon the rules and regulations of the area.

Some of the state-controlled areas are excellent, offering fine duck hunting. Others are less desirable either because of location or because of the conditions under which they are operated. But for the guy who doesn't have a great amount of time and money, they offer hunting that on average is far better, at much lower cost, than he can find on his own or by shooting commercial clubs. There are even ways in which the percentage of hunting success on these areas can be improved, assuring the knowledgeable of even better hunting than luck of the draw affords.

Most of the state-operated duck and goose areas work on an advance-reservation basis. This does not necessarily exclude those who did not have the foresight or luck to have obtained a permit for specific days. Most areas have a limited number of blinds, or shooting positions, which are given to those holding permits.

But again, not everyone holding a permit shows up, and "stand-bys" are accepted to fill out the blinds available. Even if the permit holders show in full force, most areas allow stand-bys *without* permits to re-enter or take over these blinds after the original permit holders have shot their limits. In any given area there are usually three or four blinds that are a good choice and account for the most birds, and even if he gets into one of them late, the stand-by is often better off than those whose permits placed them in a less desirable blind.

Some areas hold pre-season drawings with no other qualification than a valid hunting license. This is why some hunters provide their whole family and as many friends as possible with licenses, making them all eligible to draw. With luck, one family may even draw two or three blinds, choosing only the best of the lot and returning the rest to the pot for redrawing.

Under these conditions, it is usually expected that the drawer will build his own blind, which he will then have daily throughout the season, provided that he claims it by a certain time each morning. However, if the blind owner does not show up, the blind is open. Other areas provide the blinds and have a drawing before shooting hours each morning to assign hunters to them.

Even if you don't draw a blind, there is often a lone hunter who does. Don't be bashful—strike up a conversation and see if you can be invited along. Few people enjoy hunting alone.

Before heading for the area, make a phone call to see how large attendance at drawings has been. Also bear in mind that while many areas may be filled to capacity on weekends and holidays, almost all of them have openings during the week, especially after the season has been underway for a while.

On some state areas and, most notably, the federal areas, the supervisory personnel is highly professional. On those areas that do not use Conservation Department personnel or people who have qualified for the profession under Civil Service, you may find a man picked more as a result of political patronage than any knowledge or talent for running a shooting area.

But whether the area is run by a pro or political appointee, introduce yourself and ask sensible and discreet questions about the area. Try to find out how the shooting has been, and which blinds have produced the most. Finally, simply, honestly, and

A fairly recent system at some state-controlled shooting areas permits no permanent blind building; hunters must use natural vegetation, or bring their own camouflage material which must be removed at the end of the day.

frankly ask his advice on how best to hunt the position you have drawn. Your success or failure will often depend on his answer, for in these areas you'll find some of the best and some of the worst duck hunters known to exist.

Public areas are especially subject to sky-busting, for which no one yet has found a remedy. Don't let it bother you. Accept it as a handicap with which you'll have to live, and don't count on being able to work swinging birds to your decoys without adjacent blinds having a crack at them.

Since blinds on these areas are used by many people, no matter how well they are constructed in the beginning, they become rather sparsely camouflaged and broken-down shortly after opening day. If you can, take along a supply of the material originally used to build the blind, or extra willows, cornstalks, or anything else that will help to fill in the holes.

Also remember that many areas have restrictions on when you may enter or leave blinds. Take lunch and coffee, since you may go out at 4:30 in the morning and not return until 1:00 or later in the afternoon, regardless of your success or lack of it.

Some areas rent decoys, boat cushions, boats, and what-have-you. If you don't have your own, check this out in advance and reserve what you need, keeping in mind that any decoys you may bring will probably be superior to the cracked, broken, and paint-scraped lumps offered for rent.

Since duck hunting depends much upon the wind and its direction, it may be that some blinds are ideal for some winds and worthless in others. This is another point to check and a question to ask of someone familiar with the area.

There is an old maxim among duck hunters to the effect that "the guy in the other blind is a son-of-a-bitch." Unfortunately, this is nowhere truer than in public shooting areas. If the hunters in the adjacent blind are particularly obnoxious, you might try changing your decoy set-up to the far side of the blind, to put as much distance as you can between your birds and their blind. However, obnoxiousness is frequently due more to ignorance than to malice. When this is the case, you'll do better by making a visit to their blind, perhaps offering to share coffee or sandwiches, and at the same time subtly suggesting a change in their course

These Canadas are feeding at the Crab Orchard refuge near Carbondale, Illinois. Daily fee clubs surround many areas like this, and provide good shooting at a very reasonable cost.

of action. In my experience this works much better than shouting obscenities back and forth.

DAY SHOOTS

Day shooting is a private, commercial enterprise wherein you pay a set fee to hunt. This can mean anything from giving a farm pond owner a half-pint of booze, to shooting at a well-organized and well-run commercial club charging from $10 to $100 per day per gun. Most of the larger clubs are very well run. Their business is providing good shooting for their paying guests, and they know every trick in the book as to how to accomplish that end under sporting conditions with a minimum amount of hunter discomfort.

In these clubs you will frequently find such niceties of life as heated blinds or pits, complete with stoves for lunch-making. There may be upholstered seats, and even running water. Day shoots in clubs of this caliber usually mean that everything is furnished except your gun and ammunition. Included are large spreads of pre-set decoys, whether duck or geese, usually a guide/caller to accompany you, and perhaps a fairly well-trained retriever in the bargain.

But these are commercial enterprises. They are a business, and run as such. In some places, it is customary for the guide to shoot alongside of you, which means if you can't hit 'em, he will fill out your limit. Since few hunters enjoy taking home another man's ducks when they have paid to kill their own, it is best to simply inform the guide that you don't care how many ducks *he* kills, but they are *his* and you prefer to hit or miss your own. The guide's shooting is often done to fill out the blind's limit as quickly as possible so that another party may enter. So find out in advance whether you are renting the blind by the day or whether you are expected to shoot and get out as quickly as possible.

Sometimes commercial clubs that do a large business over-extend themselves to make room for more shooters. In other words, they place blinds too close together, or put up additional blinds in poor positions. The stranger would have small chance of knowing this in advance were it not that almost everyone around these areas is a hunter, including the waiter in the restaurant and the gas station attendant. People such as this can often be relied on for information as to which club, or which blind at a certain club, you should seek or avoid. Such preliminary detective work can save a lot of empty days.

GOOSE HUNTING ON CONTROLLED AREAS

Geese found on controlled areas cannot be considered the same bird found in the "wild," for he is a bird who has learned to live and operate within strict patterns. Just how precisely they have adjusted to these patterns can be demonstrated by their uncanny ability to tell time and judge distance.

A good illustration is the Horseshoe Lake area near Cairo, Illinois, where the regulations require shooting to be stopped at 3:00 in the afternoon. Every day at 3:05, great flocks of geese rise out of the refuge and begin their trek to the fields, though the sky may have been virtually gooseless before. As to their judgment of distance and boundaries, Horseshoe Lake has a highway skirting the perimeter of the refuge. On the refuge side of the road, geese graze so close to the highway that the wind from passing cars ruffles their feathers. There is no fence, but you won't find one goose on the other side of the road.

Around most refuges there is a controlled shooting area, but it is usually surrounded by private day-shoot clubs. From my experience and information given me, it seems that another habit of refuge geese follows much the same pattern throughout the country. Depending on the time of season, early or late, the majority of refuge geese fly out in only one direction. For example, they prefer the east side of the refuge in early season, and later, when temperatures and daylight hours diminish, they change their flight plan and from then on fly out the west side. Whether the direction they prefer is east or west, north or south, will depend upon the given area, but this is precious information for the hunter intending to shoot these areas.

Another generally held belief is that the time of your hunt to these areas should be planned to coincide with the dark of the moon. Full moons often find the birds feeding at night and returning to the refuge before dawn, to spend the day resting inside.

Whatever blind or pit you draw, on either the public or private grounds, decoys will be already set up in more or less permanent positions, to be left that way throughout the season. However, this decoy set will have gone stale for many of the birds familiar with the area, and may be placed entirely wrong for the prevailing flight or wind. Few places have rules saying that decoys cannot be repositioned, so if you have a better idea, go ahead and reposition them. In any event, at least turn the decoys to head into the wind as geese do naturally to prevent their feathers from being ruffled. But, remember, silhouettes must face in all directions for them to be seen by birds approaching from any angle.

One of those days! Sometimes the most enticing spread of decoys can't get birds away from the refuge; the boundary here is the tree line, and the Canadas sure know where it is.

While some places furnish large, luxurious spreads of fifty, sixty, or one hundred good-looking, full-bodied decoys, others provide only a half-dozen rather crude silhouettes. If you know in advance that the latter condition prevails, your hunt will turn out better if you supplement the decoys by bringing along some of your own.

TOWER DUCKS

Spread throughout our land are some 2,000 shooting preserves, the vast majority open to the public. There, by paying a set fee per bird, you may shoot ducks, pheasants, quail, chukar, etc. Many of these offer a form of duck shooting that has commonly become termed "tower mallards." These are flighted birds in a semi-wild state that have been drawn by feed to enclosed pens without water. In some cases, they are then walked up a ramp to a tower and released, one or more at a time, and being thirsty, they head directly for the nearby lake. Underneath this flight line, and often in blinds on the lake, are positioned the shoot-for-fee "hunters."

No other form of duck shooting has been so condemned by some and praised by others. As far as I'm concerned, put-and-take preserves serve a definite function and serve it well. They are an excellent place for anyone, man, woman, or child, to begin learning the rudiments of gun handling and duck hunting. They also offer those whose advanced age or other physical handicaps prevent from sloughing through the marsh a chance to continue duck shooting. Finally, they offer those whose time is limited or who do not enjoy or cannot tolerate rough hunting an opportunity to shoot ducks.

Most of those who condemn this type of shooting should open their minds and evaluate it, not as duck hunting, but as a distinctly different type of shooting, as different as skeet shooting is from quail hunting. Moreover, even the expert duck hunter can make the shooting of these "tame" birds an exacting challenge to his expertise. For tower shooting offers every conceivable kind of shot that can be found in rough hunting. The expert need not take close birds and can, in fact, with a clear conscience, stretch his skill, gun, and ammunition to its outermost limits.

Positions may be found within these flightways where only 80-yard birds need be fired at, if this is your wish. On the other hand, if you are a starting gunner you may be positioned for easy 20-25-yard shots and get an amount of practice in a day's time that might take several seasons under natural hunting conditions.

The season for these shooting preserves starts early and runs into March, and this is available both before and after the regular hunting seasons. Indeed, the late-winter conditions under which you shoot may in some respects be far sportier than those you found in regular hunting, when the season closed long before the advent of cold weather.

Since this is not duck hunting, but duck shooting, total concealment is seldom necessary, and the camaraderie that exists between several shooters in a group may express itself in wiping the other guy's eye, making bets, or taking turns for solo shooting in front of an audience of peers.

At the end of the day, all birds are retrieved, cleaned, and ready for the hunter to take home. The only problem with this type of shooting is that it can be an expensive proposition for those who get caught up in the heat of gunning, and forget to count how many ducks they are dropping—at $4 to $6 per bird! Let me also remind you to be wary when shooting with a group that suggests pro-rating the cost after shooting. It's better to know what you're getting in for.

13·
The
Duck Club

The last sanctum sanctorum of male supremacy is the duck club. There are about 6,000 of them spread unevenly across the continental United States, and they control over 3 million acres of the choicest hunting in the world.

Some states have over 1,000 clubs; others only one or two, but the term is loosely used. A club's membership may run from two buddies who have permission to shoot their neighbor's farm pond to large, long-established organizations that hold vast acreage for the use of their many members. The term is so loosely applied it covers the independently owned "shoot for daily fee" areas as well as a few clubs whose membership is now limited to inheritance.

Equally wide divergence can be found in the rules of each club, and behavior expected of its members, but all have one thing in common—they are a gathering of the clan, a place for men of good fellowship to pursue the sport of ducking. A properly run duck club has so much to offer compared to today's posted lands and crowded "free" hunting areas that the club is thought, by most experienced hunters, to be the best of all worlds.

CHOOSING A CLUB

Each duck club has its own character, a composite of the personalities of its members. And for this reason your choice of a club depends heavily on your own temperament, experience, and favorite way of hunting. Of course, as in most of life, the choice is also usually dictated by economics. And this, in turn, is often determined by area. Clubs readily accessible from large metropolitan areas may be expensive and snobbish to the point of choosing their members only from certain walks of life, with dues high enough to discourage the "rabble." But these are exceptions, for seldom is democracy better portrayed than in most duck-club memberships. Members entering the portals of the

Clubhouse and outbuildings of the famous Duck Island Gun Club, near Banner, Illinois, a favorite shooting ground of the legendary Fred Kimble, perhaps the greatest duck shot who ever lived.

club leave their business and social rank outside. So the choice is yours—one you can wisely make with certain considerations.

Once you've determined that a club's membership is to your liking, it is best to let your desires be known and try to wangle an invitation to shoot. Only in this way can you better come to know the individuals and the type of shooting offered. Here your general health enters the picture. Some clubs are easy hunting while others require strenuous exertion. As remarked before, the distance you must travel to get to the club is another prime consideration. If you have free time and the club offers living facilities, you may, as many do, stay for several days at a time. But if you are limited to Sunday shooting, it becomes a drag to have to rise at 2:00 or 3:00 in the morning in order to be on the marsh at sunrise.

WHAT DOES IT COST—REALLY?

Sometimes there are hidden costs in club shooting. For example, dues are known, but assessments often are not. What are the future plans for your club? Do they include extensive building or repairs and, if so, what will you be expected to cough up at that time? Another consideration is the amount and type of equipment you'll need to compete with other members. Will your present decoys, boat, and motor suffice, or will you need more and different equipment at greater cost? Most clubs pro-rate the cost of their caretaker (if any) as well as daily living expenses.

Just what are you getting for your money? Does it purchase only shooting privileges for that season, or does it include an actual share of club assets? Some clubs are "working" clubs in which members do all the work, while others hire to get it done. Find out what it costs. There is a difference in being able to pay for a thing and being able to afford it.

HOW GOOD IS THE HUNTING?

The most important aspect is whether the hunting itself is worth it. How does your intended club rate, in birds per man per season, with adjacent clubs charging the same dues? Of course, this cannot be determined on the basis of one season's kill alone; there may be extenuating circumstances and a club cannot be fairly rated by a single poor (or good) season.

One's own experience and preference in type of duck shooting should enter strongly into your choice. Some hunters derive their greatest enjoyment from working birds over the decoys, while others don't care for close ducks and consider long-range pass shooting the ultimate in wildfowling. Some clubs offer only large, open-water blinds where a variety of ducks, both puddle and divers, are taken. Others are pothole purists who delight in timber shooting. It's a lucky club that offers both.

The clubhouse of Jimmy Robinson's Sports Afield Duck Club on Manitoba's Delta Marsh, as it looked before it was replaced by a more modern structure. Clark Gable and Robert Taylor—both of whom knew what to do with a shotgun—were among the famous personalities who occupied its chicken-wire-sprung beds.

An advantage of clubs is the fact that pro-rated costs enable the members to use equipment like this Hustler ATV that might be prohibitively expensive for the individual.

My own experience suggests that the happiest clubs are run by membership vote among reasonable-minded gentlemen. But many are dominated by a single person, perhaps the owner of the land, whose views on hunting may be entirely different from your own.

STARTING A CLUB

While I strongly recommend you belong to an existing club for several seasons first, circumstances may suggest your starting your own club. This is especially true in clubless areas, or those in which existing clubs are prohibitive in price or closed to new membership.

Your first step is to find a few compatible, but clubless, hunters. Through an informal meeting you determine the amount of money available. Then it becomes a matter of finding, leasing, or buying a piece of suitable ground or water. Again, depending on your location, this could be easy, difficult, or well nigh impossible.

Finding land

Ask help from club owners, wardens, and old hunters in your area. Most of them know what land is available and whether or not it is worthwhile. Real-estate people are seldom helpful, since few know what constitutes good duck property.

Leasing

Nose around and ask questions. Often owners of farmland can be talked into yearly leasing. You may be lucky enough to find an existing club ready to disband, or a good chunk of land for a long-term lease.

In leasing, as in all legal matters, an attorney's fee is cheap insurance, no matter what it costs. The non-legal mind is sure to overlook vital facts such as liability, subleasing, and correctly defining limitations. Of course, it is up to you to make your wishes known. What do you propose doing about eventual ownership of outbuildings, improvements, lease renewal, or options to buy? What happens if the duck season is closed; and what has the owner promised you? Check around to find the right lawyer —he might trade his fees for a few hunts.

Assuming that you find land and can afford it, it again becomes a matter of taste and money as to the next step. The small boy in all duck hunters wants a clubhouse. But this should be secondary. Your first thoughts and expenditures may, of necessity, go into the land. Are dikes or levees needed to maintain water levels, will pumps be needed, or wells dug to get water? What duck-food crops now exist or can legally be raised? And is the land small enough to sow by hand, or is it so massive that aerial seeding is the only answer?

Improving the marsh

Few people buy a duck marsh and leave it as found. There is something in us that says we can improve it. The most common thought is to cut new flyways by removing brush or trees, a thought that surely has lessened the desirability of more areas than it has improved. Natural flyways are *always* best, and whatever our knowledge of any species of duck, we are seldom able to choose better pathways of flight than the bird now uses. Even more difficult than changing flyways is the creation of new ones, and the record of success in turning a formerly duckless area into

My home away from home—the clubhouse in the background is "Twin Springs" near Manito, Illinois, my home-base club for more than fifteen years.

a waterfowl haven is extremely poor. In fact, I would say it can be done only by the extensive use of feed, a method which presents its own set of problems, of which more later.

The clubhouse

Once your land is in shape to receive your hoped-for migratory guests, thoughts can turn to housing. This is where your original choice of members makes a big difference. In my opinion, a six-member duck club should ideally consist of a carpenter, an electrician, a sporting-goods dealer, a lumberyard owner, a lawyer, and a liquor distributor. If you can't get all six, try for as many categories as possible—they'll come in handy, whether there is an existing dwelling or you intend to build. But many clubs find that overnight accommodations are not required. A shack in which to warm up, change clothes, and have a bite to eat is often adequate and sometimes charming. And this can often be done at small expense through the purchase of an old trailer, pre-fab garage, or garden house.

Perhaps you can arrange to rent a farm outbuilding near your shooting grounds, which is not as unhandy as it sounds if you can find a way to secure your equipment on the marsh. How heavily you must secure your equipment depends on your locality. In some areas it can be left in the open and in others it is risky to turn your back. Boats may be safeguarded for short periods by chaining them to large trees. Make sure the chain is large enough and the lock heavy enough to keep it from being easily cut or shot off. Key locks are best; combination types are hard to manipulate in the dark of morn. One of the slickest ways to protect decoys is to purchase a couple of 55-gallon drums with locking tops which can be chained to trees. They will even take a small outboard motor.

DUCK-CLUB RULES

Many clubs, especially those of small membership, seem to operate quite nicely on mutual agreements which are well understood though unspoken, a happy state of affairs seldom possible when the membership is large. In most cases it is probably wise to have a few written rules, but the fewer the better. These generally include the days of the week on which the club will shoot, as well as the hours. It also should contain provisions concerning sky-busting, unnecessary movement around the blinds and grounds, perhaps even time of day for entering or leaving blinds, use of alcohol except at specified times, and the curbing of untrained or overambitious dogs. Clubhouse privileges and responsibilities should be pointed out. Also, the method of choosing who will shoot which blinds, when, and with whom. Rules should carefully define restricted shooting areas, if any, and the use of communal equipment.

Guests

Probably the touchiest subject concerning duck clubs in general is that of guest privileges. Any rulings should certainly be discussed at length by all members, and a happy medium drawn that all can live with. Personally, I would not belong to a club that did not allow guest shooting. Most hunters are proud of their club and enjoy sharing it with close friends, even though they may not be expert hunters. On the other hand, there is constant grumbling among some memberships because of one or two men who believe they are entitled to bring as many guests as often as they wish, whether or not it crowds the hunting of dues-paying members. However, there certainly should be some provision for a member to entertain not only social friends but business associates he would like to "treat" to a duck hunt.

In order to keep this from getting out of hand, many clubs set a three or more guest per season ruling. Still others set a limit or leave it open, yet charge the host a guest fee of $10 or $25 per gun. I've never seen this ruling meet with complete approval because the sum paid per guest may be insignificant to one member while prohibitive to another. Probably the best general rule would be no guests on days of heavy traffic, such as Saturdays and Sundays.

Few men enjoy hunting more than when accompanied by their sons, but this, too, can be a problem. Hardly anyone wants to restrict a man from taking his boy hunting, but in large families of several boys it can become a burden to other members. This is sometimes resolved by setting special-rate family memberships, if the club can accommodate them.

The club set-up also affords safe storage and handy access to equipment, less crowded and more comfortable hunting conditions than in public areas, in most cases, and best of all, a camaraderie that can last a lifetime.

In general, the guests that prove most welcome and cast the least reflection upon their host are those who come, not empty-handed, but prepared in some way to reimburse the entire membership for their courtesy. This can be as simple as a bottle of booze or an invitation to the membership at large to join the guest in some activity for which he is well equipped, such as quail shooting or bass fishing.

THE MARSH MASTER

Few clubs of any type can be run by the board of directors or members at large. Most have a president, or at least someone who can be turned to for final decisions. The same holds true for duck clubs, and the post is generally filled by a marsh master, who achieves that position either by vote or general acceptance. If successful in this position, he is usually of outwardly mild temperament, inherently a diplomat, a wise old hunter by experience, and a leader of men by desire. And it should be his responsibility to sniff the morning air, judge direction of the wind, and correctly (more times than not) advise the placing of decoys, give the direction from which the ducks will work, and, in general, supervise the day's shoot. In fact, his job starts much before opening day with decisions as to the location of blinds, vegetation to be cut, and feed to be grown.

"FARMING"

There is a big difference between "baiting" and the growing of natural foods attractive to wildfowl. In most areas clubs with acreage, which do not rely on pass shooting alone, plant and grow some crop of duck food. According to the geographic area this can be millet, flooded standing corn, rice, and many different weeds and grasses.

The type of crop best suited for your use can be found by consulting other clubs and your local agricultural agent. However, it is a sticky proposition, full of pitfalls for the inexperienced and ill-informed. Before making any plantings be sure to read carefully all state and federal regulations, and to get advice from your state's Department of Conservation. Where crops can be legally grown and shot over they can be a great asset. But such shooting must be wisely done to prevent "burning out" the birds, as well as to stay within the law.

BAITING

Not all clubs do operate according to the letter of the law. Many find ways around the law, despite constant surveillance. A few clubs seem to delight in making violation a game between their members and the wardens. Illegal feeding is carried out in many ways.

Large-scale baiting of waterfowl is said to have begun in Illinois. And it is estimated that 6 million bushels of corn were dumped by that state's duck clubs during the season of 1933, the last year in which the use of bait was legal. Since laws change, it is not the purpose of this book to define what constitutes legal and illegal feeding other than to say that "baiting" or "feeding" means adding grains, grasses, or other duck foods over and above those grains or grasses which naturally grow in an area.

There are many attractive duck foods, depending on the geographic location, but corn figures most prominently in illegal baiting in territories in which this practice is most prevalent. It is one of the most desired duck foods; its yellow kernels are easily seen and found by the birds, and much needed by them in severe cold weather. The illegal baiters use such subterfuge as the "duck dish." This often takes the form of a 2x4 frame, one yard square, with a bottom of screening or wire mesh. This is sunk in shallow water, usually in the late afternoon, filled with corn, and removed in the morning before shooting time. Corn is often soaked overnight before being placed in the duck dish so it will sink and the kernels remain confined.

Some clubs buy vast quantities of weed seeds which are soaked before dumping on club grounds, and their members shoot secure in the belief that the wardens will not be able to prove the bait is other than natural. Other clubs have been known to take the attitude of baiting openly and shooting hard until they are caught and closed. Then they gladly accept such small fines as are usually handed out by local magistrates.

However, any club using extensive baiting will be caught eventually because the ducks themselves will inform on it. Any experienced observer watching the flight pattern of birds over club lands can determine in a short time whether or not feed is being used. The whole principle of baiting relies on getting the birds to find the feed and then return to it regularly. Once this has been done, the flight approach and landing of birds become markedly different. They no longer show the usual circling and indecisiveness that is natural to them when approaching unfamiliar areas, or when they need to search out food. Rather, they head to it directly and show no hesitation to drop in where feed is known to be.

Even if the club succeeds in avoiding prosecution on baiting charges, the chances are that they'll get socked with something else. There are so many laws that it is impossible to hunt indefinitely without being at least in technical violation of one law or another. While the warden may overlook, or at least not search out, some of these technical violations on clubs whose members show good intent otherwise, it is not hard for them to find you in some violation if they make it a point to do so.

Baiting is not only illegal, it is unsportsmanlike. It can be very costly in money, bad publicity, and the closing of your club, yet it is unnecessary if your club's members are hunters worthy of the name. Baiting is bad news all the way around. It reflects not only on the club so doing, but on the club's neighbors who may obey the letter of the law.

THE CLUB'S CONTRIBUTION TO THE SPORT

In the book *Waterfowl Tomorrow* (U. S. Department of the Interior), John Anderson and Frank Kozlik point out, "The contribution that duck clubs make and can make has not been appreciated fully by the Federal Government, the states, and the clubs themselves. . . . Duck clubs preserve and maintain valuable habitat, but their primary purpose is to furnish hunting. Without the incentive of reasonable seasons and bag limits, many would quit operating. Their lands lose their high value and are then converted to other uses. More waterfowl habitat is thus lost. Because state and federal agencies can never hope to own and manage enough habitat to insure waterfowl populations adequate for hunting or bird watching, private land owners must be encouraged in every practical way, short of over-harvesting, to preserve their waterfowl habitat."

And this about sums it up. Clubs with hundreds of thousands of dollars invested to assure their members of good hunting cannot be expected to maintain the burden of such expense unless they get a reasonable return in length of season and daily limits.

In many areas the hunter without club affiliations who depends upon state or federal areas for hunting would have little sport were it not for large private holdings in the same area. It is an old, but true, maxim, "Nothing helps duck hunting like ducks." Most state and federal areas are simply not large enough to provide rest and refuge for the birds and still leave room for open hunting. And unless there are resting areas where they are undisturbed, waterfowl will not stay in an area very long.

The federal government's official stand on private duck clubs has not been particularly favorable. And this is perhaps due to the fact that federal wardens make required reports only on clubs violating the law by overshooting, illegal feeding, or violation of shooting hours. There are no official reports on those clubs setting more stringent limitations on their members than the law requires. Many clubs voluntarily restrict their shooting to certain days of the week, often forbidding afternoon shooting, and in some cases make their daily bag limit less than that legally allowed in their flyway. The American duck club is of help to all wildfowlers, members or not.

14·
The Bird
in Hand

L et's say you've dropped a duck. What you do with it next determines how good it will be on the table. Many hunters just toss the bird into the boat. If it's cold weather, that's probably as good a treatment as any. But let's say that it's early in the season, and the weather is warm. Then it's a good idea to rub off the breast feathers, exposing the skin for quicker cooling. Some even prefer to gut the bird immediately.

The thing you don't want to do with game is pile it up. Whether you're going to semi-clean your bird at once or leave it alone, make sure it is separated from other dead birds. The quicker you can cool the flesh and body cavity, the fresher-tasting the meat; so it is not too bad an idea to pick or gut it so long as you keep the bird above bilge water and away from the dogs.

Though I've seen it done, it is certainly not a good idea to disembowel your bird and swish it around in the drink. If you feel better once the innards are out, simply let it go at that.

My usual method in cool weather is to hang birds by the neck in the fork of a willow or other small tree, thus getting them up and away from dog harm or contamination. But once you have them back at camp, some work is in order. This is sometimes unpleasant because the hour is late, your belly empty, and fingers numb.

214

CLEANING AND PROCESSING

If you have a lot of ducks, don't be greedy. There is little meat on a duck other than the breast. Pick and rub the breast feathers off the bird. Take a pair of game shears, kitchen scissors, or tin snips and run the point into the soft part of the belly directly under the breastbone. Now cut completely around the breast, discarding the rest of the carcass. This entire operation takes about three minutes. The snipped breasts may be prepared in any manner you would use to prepare a complete duck carcass, except that you allow a shorter baking or cooking time. If ducks are few, however, it makes a better appearance to serve the complete animal.

While reams have been written on duck plucking, complete with instructions for paraffining, steaming, and mechanical pickers, I have yet to see a more simple or better method than simply using the thumb and forefinger and picking the duck in the age-old manner. This should be done before the duck is gutted for convenience and less messiness.

Once the ducks are plucked and gutted I like to soak them in several rinses of salt water, simply to remove blood, and not, as most people believe, take away the "gamy" flavor. A good duck has a game flavor and that's what makes it taste like a duck.

If your club is fortunate enough to have a freezer, snipped breasts are best kept in milk cartons filled with water. In a properly set freezer they will keep in this manner for well over a year with no sign of drying out or freezer burn. However, law-abiding citizens should check the possession regulations each year to determine just how long game may be legally kept.

The whole carcass may also be frozen after being wrapped individually in freezer foil, but it is then best used within thirty to ninety days. Otherwise, it will be found to be extremely dry and show the effects of burn.

Many clubs without freezer facilities build a dry-box—simply an enclosure that is insect- and rodent-free, in which game may be left to season. This, too, bears watching, as ducks that freeze, thaw, and are refrozen by the weather rapidly lose appeal even though they become somewhat tenderized.

However, almost every camp has an icebox or refrigerator, and your birds are best kept in it with light wrapping, and in a bowl to catch blood.

Today, when hunting is often done on a daily basis and the hunter returns to the city at the end of the day, birds may be taken to commercial pickers. They must be tagged with the hunter's name, amount, and the species of duck, satisfying the law and seemingly assuring the hunter of getting back his own birds. In practice, this is often a false surmise and he may as likely wind up with two bluebills as with two canvasbacks.

Even worse, his game is usually tossed into a pile on the picker's floor and left there for several hours, if not days, until the "steam gang" gets around to them. During the Thanksgiving holidays, this may be a long period indeed, as most commercial pickers are primarily poultry houses.

Those picking their own know they are their own and how they were treated. If large numbers of birds are regularly picked, a club can sometimes find bargains in used mechanical pickers whose rapidly whirling rubber fingers flog off feathers quickly and easily. There are also smaller versions on the market at reasonable cost and designed with the sportsman in mind.

Shipping game is even more risky. Modern express companies are known for speedy-sounding mottos and snail-slow deliveries, at higher and higher costs. My experience over the past decade suggests that the hunter who cannot bring back his own birds would be better off in every way by becoming known as a fine fellow who distributes his take among the natives of the area in which he was hunting.

No matter how they are packed, birds shipped home seldom get there in edible condition. Dry ice burns and dries them to a crisp, while wet ice melts and leaves only soggy lumps of decaying flesh.

Some still prefer to let their ducks hang to ripen and I suppose they know what they like, but a couple of days in the home refrigerator is enough for my taste. The better care you take of birds in the field, the better they taste on the table.

CAMP COOKIN'

Great recipes of game cookery are esteemed throughout the

world. They include some of the most involved forms of food preparation known to master chefs at the fanciest restaurants. Pressed duck is a good example. (A duck press may be had for only $250-$350 at today's prices.) The French believe the duck should be suffocated so as to lose no blood. Certainly Mandarin and Peking ducks have a following, but they ain't what the boys eat down at the duck club.

In camp, hunters like their food straight and simple. The rule of thumb is to fry it in grease, use plenty of onions, and serve it with potatoes. Fancy stuff is out! Anything that can be cooked in one pot saves dishwashing, even though it's an unwritten law the cook never dips his hands into soapy water. That alone should be enough reward for learning the following basic recipes, which will bail you out if you're elected camp cook.

By the way, when you get that post, you'll often be asked what you're serving. It's always best to pick a name with a distant, but familiar, sound to it. If you are cooking on the Texas Gulf, say, "Hell, that's Delta Marsh Mulligan." If you're in a Canadian camp, tell 'em it's "Stuttgart Stew."

The following recipes are basic. They are duck recipes for people who enjoy eating duck. Most are as simple as frying a hamburger and can be cooked while you and the boys enjoy a nip of Old Loudmouth.

Few ovens in camp have a thermometer, and in those that do, it's stopped working. A "hot" oven is 400°-500°, moderate, 350°-375°. For cooking time, feel your way along by the tenderness of bird and degree of rarity that suits your taste.

Roast duck

If you have plump, grain-fed birds and like roast duck, the following will result in as good as you'll get.

Ingredients:
One duck
Half apple
Small whole onion per man

Rub the bird inside and out with salt and pepper. Shove the half apple and peeled onions inside. Roast in a hot oven on roasting-pan rack for 1¼ hours (longer for well done—poke with fork to see if blood is running). Baste several times with butter and cheap red wine. (Throw away the apple and onions before serving duck.)

Moist roast duck

Stuff duck with apple and onions, as in previous recipe, then baste with 50-50 mixture butter/vermouth. Wrap tightly in heavy foil; bake one hour at moderate heat. Open foil, baste, and bake another 20 minutes. This method retains moisture in the flesh and overcomes the complaint of those who call duck dry.

Fried duck

Here is a great way to fix young mallard, wood duck, and especially teal.

Skin them; cut large but thin slices of breast. Boil in 50-50 mixture of orange juice and water about 10 or 15 minutes. Add more water if it boils off. Remove slices of duck, and fry in butter until brown.

Fried goose breast

Young goose or old, this recipe guarantees tender eating.

Cut breast off carcass and sprinkle with salt, pepper, and flour. Hammer breast thin and flat with empty bottle. Slowly brown in well-buttered skillet. Cover with white wine (sauterne or Rhine) and simmer breasts until tender.

Broiled duck

Some claim duck is too dry to ever be broiled. Try this and be the judge.

Cut out and use only breast, but leave on bone. Rub with butter, salt, pepper, and wrap with bacon strips. Shove under broiler and keep basting with mixture of melted butter and orange juice until done.

Old honker stew

Stews are always great camp favorites and if cooked long enough, they can hardly go wrong.

Cut meat of old honker from carcass in cubes. Sprinkle with flour, salt, and pepper; brown in bacon grease in large heavy skillet. Add chopped onion, parsley, carrots, and water to cover.

Simmer 45 minutes. Add quartered potatoes and give it another half-hour. Before serving, stir in a tablespoon of Worcestershire.

Roaster duck with sauerkraut

Club members should chip in for an electric roaster. Its timed and controlled heat makes all cooking a pleasure. Turn it on when leaving for blind, and dinner will be ready on return. The following roaster recipe makes for a "moist" duck which many prefer.

Rub ducks with salt and pepper, lots of it. Blend with sauerkraut, plenty of butter and quartered apples. Dump everything, including kraut juice, over ducks and set roaster at 400°-425°.

Mudhen

As a kid, my old man and I had an understanding—I *must* eat everything I shot. After an engagement with a hell-diver (grebe), this rule provided solid protection for many creatures of the marsh, but led directly to my taste for mudhen.

So far as I can see, there are only two reasons why coot rate such low esteem on the table. The first is that few modern hunters know how to clean them; and second, that fewer still know whether they are to be baked, broiled, fried, or roasted.

There is a small, but important, secret in both steps. You don't pluck a mudhen, you skin it. This is easily done by laying the bird on its back, head forward and wings outstretched.

Plant one foot on each wing, grab the bird's feet, and pull strongly upward to split the carcass. This will pull away the breast and leave behind the back and intestines. It is now easy to remove the breast skin and feathers with your thumb and forefinger, and the breast is all you eat of the coot.

The mudhen is strongly vegetarian and far tastier than many breeds of ducks. The gamy taste is mostly in the fat, which should be removed as completely as possible.

The old-timers liked to plop a coot breast into a pan of sizzling butter to brown and then cube into it a vegetable stew of onion, red wine, garlic, bay leaves, and a generous chunk of salt pork. A two-hour simmer of this conglomeration has warmed bellies and hearts in many a duck club.

But if your taste tends toward less gamy fare, marinate the breasts in the refrigerator overnight in the juice of a couple of lemons, a cup of water, some red wine, garlic, and bay leaves.

They should then be lightly browned and all the fat and grease drained off. Then add a few slices of bacon and a cup of the marinade. Put a lid on the pot and simmer for a couple of hours. When the breasts are removed, thicken the remaining marinade in the pan with flour and serve it over the breasts, accompanied by peas and potatoes.

Trash duck marinade

Good ducks don't need to be soaked in strong salt water or baking soda. But maybe all the boys could bring down were a few trash ducks. In this case, clean as usual and marinate them overnight in a mixture of half vinegar and half water, to which a slice of onion, sliced clove of garlic, a couple of bay leaves and cloves, and salt and pepper have been added. Next day, the birds can be roasted or put in a stew.

Cumberland sauce

A sauce based on oranges and currant jelly is widely known as "Cumberland Sauce." Read twenty game cookbooks and you'll get as many variations on the recipe. Being particularly fond of this sauce, I've tried many formulas before settling on the following, given me by my old hunting partner, Jack Brunnenmeyer.

Ingredients:
½ cup Karo white syrup
½ cup currant jelly
½ tsp. dry mustard
3 oranges, of which you juice two and slice one very thin—peel and all.

Bring everything to a boil and simmer it about 20 minutes. Then add ½ stick of butter and cook until melted. Serve it over either duck or goose.

Wild rice

Side dishes and dressings are a matter of choice, but wild rice is a classic and traditional accompaniment.

Chop livers and gizzards; boil for 15 minutes. Stir wild rice into water; cook until tender. Fry some chopped onions, green peppers, celery in butter until soft. Pour rice into pan, mix, and serve.

15.
Rules
of the Game

All games have rules and sometimes duck hunting seems to have more than its share. Federal migratory-bird hunting regulations change almost annually and differ according to the flyway. State hunting laws not only vary but are often applicable only to certain counties. It is the duty of the individual to make himself aware of what the law allows and prohibits, and to adhere to the law scrupulously.

You should obtain a copy of your state regulations when you renew your hunting license, and keep it with your hunting gear. It will list the official hours at which shooting can start and must stop, and much other essential information. You should also obtain a copy of the federal regulations, which can usually be obtained from your state Fish and Game Commission, or if not, by writing directly to the Director, Fish and Wildlife Service, Department of the Interior, Washington, D.C. 20240.

Every duck hunter must carry on his person both a valid current state hunting license and a federal duck stamp, duly signed across the face. The duck stamp, which provides funds for marshland acquisition, improvement, and maintenance within the continental limits of the United States, has an interesting history. Originally, there was severe opposition to all federal intervention

A collector's page of the first twelve years of duck stamps. They were issued under the auspices of the Department of Agriculture unil 1939, then under the Department of the Interior from that date to the present.

in wildfowling activities, so much so that the first federal game law of 1913 was overturned as unconstitutional. It was not until 1918 that the "Enabling Act" finally spelled doom for market hunting and the wholesale slaughter of ducks and geese.

The Duck Stamp Act went into effect on July 1, 1934, and required anyone past the age of sixteen to obtain one in order to hunt waterfowl. The purpose of the act was to provide money to acquire and reclaim what little marshland was left. From 1934 to 1966, some $94 million in stamp money purchased over a half-million acres of refuge, plus a quarter-million acres of nesting area. Much of this land is open to hunting today, but would have been gobbled up by private interests if the money had not been available from the sale of stamps.

This is where the duck-stamp money goes—to create heart-warming scenes like this one, shot at the J. Clark Solger National Wildlife Refuge near Minot, North Dakota.

Incidentally, the stamp itself has always been among the most beautiful issued—not only because of the subject matter, but also because of the interest taken in the design by many talented outdoor artists. Originally, only the best-known painters of wildlife were invited to submit designs, but it is now a contest open to the public. Any artist may enter in any medium he chooses: oil, watercolor, tempera, or ink, but it must be 5 by 7 inches in size and in black and white only. Judging is by a committee of artists and waterfowl authorities. The winner receives only an album with a plate-sheet of the stamp he designed, plus the honor and publicity.

UNWRITTEN RULES

In addition to the state and federal regulations, there is a very old wildfowling tradition that embodies certain unwritten rules that are quite as important, in practice, as those found in the legal statutes. None of these is more important than the code covering the safe handling of firearms:

You **must always**—

make sure your gun cannot possibly fall down while it is leaning or lying at rest; and

keep all mud, snow, or other obstructions out of your barrel.

You **must not**—

ever, under any circumstance, point either a loaded or unloaded gun toward anyone at any time;

load your gun until you are in the blind and ready to shoot;

hand your gun to anyone muzzle first;

take the safety off until you are ready to shoot;

mix different gauge shells in your pocket; or

shoot over anyone's head.

In addition to the rules of safety that everyone **must** follow, there are unwritten rules of sportsmanlike conduct that are almost as important:

You **should not**—

claim you hit a certain bird when others are shooting too;

always try to get off the first shot;

make lengthy excuses for missing;

always grab the best shooting position in the blind or boat;

choose the best birds, when dividing the bag;

give instructions to or discipline another man's dog;

continuously blow a call when no birds are present;

keep resetting your decoys when birds are moving and others are hunting close by;

refuse to give all possible assistance in retrieving dead or crippled birds, even if shot from another blind; or

pick up another man's gun without his permission.

"OUTLAWING"

Most of us who outlawed as a kid eventually learned that hunting is no fun when you have to keep looking over your shoulder. However, I've known adults who still cling to the outdated attitude of the old-time market hunter—the attitude proclaiming that ducks belong to those who can take them, in any manner and amount they need or desire.

I was part of such a group, many years ago. I hunted with them and recall how proudly they unloaded their boat of eighty birds when the legal limit was a generous dozen. Game wardens were appointed from among them—most likely on the theory it takes a thief to catch one—but the only violators they arrested were "outsiders." Although many of the group worked as guides and pushers, smilingly taking the greenhorn's money and drinking his whiskey, they held only contempt for the foreigners who followed the rules of law and sportsmanship. Those who took meager pay as watchmen for big-city clubs would either rent out or invite friends to shoot on the "rest days" when club members were absent. And whatever game laws were in effect were unknown or did not apply to them. Such laws were made only for sport hunters.

Sadly, this attitude still exists around some ducking areas of the country. Such thinking with respect to regulation and limitation is of long standing, and, like racism, will possibly never be completely erased in one generation. Many are "good ol' boys" but their time has gone and we can no longer afford their predation on the ever decreasing supply of ducks.

Waterfowl follow natural cycles of scarcity and abundance, but outside factors increasingly affect these cycles. Bag limits in general and those applied to certain species in particular are set to provide hunting without drastically reducing duck population. The hunter who bends the rules in only small ways is even more dangerous than "the group," because he is more numerous. If every duck-stamp purchaser shot only *one* illegal bird per season, the total would be 2 million birds over and above our annual legal bag. We can't afford it, and the birds can't stand it.

We are *not* going to see a substantial increase in our duck population. There is no way we can make it happen. Hunting pressure will increase, and breeding areas become smaller. If we are to have ducks in huntable numbers for the future, each of us must do everything possible to conserve what we have now by hunting within the rules of sportsmanship and those established by law. The next time you are tempted to shoot after hours or take an extra bird, multiply your offense by 2 million when considering its effect on the sport.

That ought to make you think a bit. And while you're thinking, consider the fact that although 85 percent of our ducks are raised in Canada, your duck-stamp money cannot be used to purchase nesting grounds outside the United States. Then pull out your checkbook and write a check to Ducks Unlimited. It's not, strictly speaking, a "rule of the game" but if I had my druthers, it would be; for every man, woman, and child who cares about wildlife in general, not to mention wildfowl in particular, ought to belong to DU, as it's popularly called.

DUCKS UNLIMITED

Ducks Unlimited is the waterfowl hunters' own organization, with close to 95,000 members. Their primary concern is to keep the "duck factory" operating. The duck factory is the great Canadian prairie breeding grounds where the majority of our ducks are raised. This area is subject to drought, flood, and predation by both man and nature.

If ducks are to be maintained in huntable numbers, these nesting areas must be saved and protected from the advance and pressure of population growth which in time would drain them for farming and other uses. The over $36 million contributed by DU members is preserving land, as well as reclaiming large areas already lost. Such money builds dams and dikes and controls water to assure adequate conditions for duck breeding and nesting even when nature does not.

Ducks Unlimited is a nonpolitical, nonprofit organization. Throughout America its over 600 chapters hold annually what have become known as DU rallies. These take the form of dinners or open-to-the-public, pre-season get-togethers where all hunters and their families, members or not, view the latest in wildfowling equipment, and are advised on latest regulations. Many chapters also conduct duck-calling and decoy championships.

Membership in DU includes a subscription to *Ducks Unlimited* magazine, helping the interested hunter keep abreast of latest developments in equipment, legislation, and what is happening in general to our waterfowl. All duck hunters should make a DU membership as much a part of their gear as a gun and shells. Make it a point to contact your local DU chapter or write for information to Ducks Unlimited, Box 66300, Chicago, Illinois 60666.

DUCK TALK

I suppose it's not even an unwritten rule that duck hunters ought to talk like duck hunters (when they're not talking like ducks, through a call)—but it's handy to understand some of the more commonly used terms, a few of which are listed below. Of course, the whole language is too big to transcribe, with all of its regional variants (and its generous seasoning of profanity), but almost any veteran waterfowler will know what the following mean:

"Arkansas" To shoot into a group of ducks on the water.

brace A pair of bagged ducks.

cannon Usually applied to 10-gauge magnum guns.

confidence decoy Usually a heron, seagull, or crow decoy set near duck decoys.

dickybird Any bird flying by that is not a game bird.

driving Chasing ducks toward gunners by means of a power boat or vehicle.

drop-ins Ducks seemingly appearing from nowhere that are not noticed until over or in your decoys.

early starter A gunner who shoots before legal hours.

feather boat A brush-camouflaged boat.

fill out To limit out—get your limit.

flock-shooting Shooting into a flock of flying ducks without aiming at any particular bird.

funnel To drop rapidly from high altitude.

gaggle Flock of geese when on the water.

ground-swat Shoot into a group of ducks on the water.

horse cock A duck call attached to an accordion-pleated rubber hose and shaken to sound a call.

kicker Outboard motor.

knob Two or more wigeon.

lay-out boat Low-profile, punt-type skiff often camouflaged as a floating blind.

loose oars Oars run through a ring or U-shaped oarlock and not directly connected to it.

new ducks Migrating birds that have just come into the area.

pick-up Retrieval of decoys at the end of hunting.

plug Wooden or plastic rod placed in the magazine of a repeating shotgun to limit the number of shells to two in magazine and one in chamber, in conformance with federal regulations.

posted land Land that has been posted with "No Hunting or Trespassing" signs.

pothole Small pond or body of water.

punt Small duck boat.

pusher Guide.

raft Mass of ducks, when sitting together on open water.

rag spread White rags, diapers, newspapers, etc., used in decoying snow geese.

salted Illegally baited.

sawbill Merganser.

scow A flat-bottomed boat, often called a mud scow.

sheldrake Merganser.

skein Flock of flying geese.

sky-busting Shooting out of range.

slough Marsh.

sookie Hen mallard.

sord A flight of more than two mallards.

spread A number of decoys set out for hunting.

stomping Despicable action of driving less desirable species of ducks already shot into the mud bottom so that the hunter may continue shooting and be "within his limit."

stool A number of decoys set out for hunting (derived from the term "stool pigeon"). Also used as a verb.

susies Hen mallards.

tank Small pond or reservoir.

team Several ducks on the wing.

tight oars Oars connected directly to the oarlock, easier for the amateur to use but more likely to produce blisters than loose ones.

trash ducks Species less desirable for table use, such as mergansers and shovelers.

wavy Snow goose.

whiftling An action sometimes taken by flocks of geese where individual birds of the group perform aerial acrobatics.

white spread Same as "rag spread."

yellow dent Corn.

Appendix A: Bibliography

The books listed below, both new and old, are regarded by the author as classics in the field of waterfowling. Several are long out of print but may be found in larger libraries or obtained through the listing of book dealers.

BARBER, JOEL. *Wild Fowl Decoys*. Windward House, 1934.
(Also later Dover edition. The classic book on collecting decoys.)

BERNSEN, PAUL S. *The North American Waterfowler*. Salisbury Press, 1972.
(A modern "how-to." Informative, with emphasis on West Coast hunting.)

BRUETTE, WILLIAM A. *American Duck, Goose and Brant Shooting*. G. H. Watt, 1929. (Also later Scribner editions. An excellent work by a former editor of *Forest & Stream*.)

CARTIER, JOHN O. *Getting the Most Out of Waterfowling*. St. Martins, 1973.
(A solid contemporary account by a thoroughly proficient Michigan wildfowler.)

CONNETT, EUGENE. *Duck Shooting Along the Atlantic Tidewater*. Morrow, 1947. (Also later Bonanza edition.)

CONNETT, EUGENE. *Wildfowling in the Mississippi Flyway*. D. Van Nostrand, 1949.
(Both volumes above are collections of stories by old-time

hunters, "gentleman" and professional. All knew their ducking well and have written interesting and informative articles.)

GRESHAM, GRITS. *The Complete Wildfowler*. Winchester Press, 1973.

(Excellent instruction is given in an easy-to-read manner in this modern "how to" by a much-traveled, highly capable author and gunner.)

GRINNELL, G. B. *American Duck Shooting*. Forest & Stream Pub. Co., 1901.

(How it was and how it was done at the beginning of the century.)

HEILNER, VAN CAMPEN. *A Book on Duck Shooting*. Alfred A. Knopf, 1947.

(In the opinion of many, the best duck-hunting book ever written.)

HINMAN, BOB. *The Golden Age of Shotgunning*. Winchester Press, 1971.

(The complete story of the American shotgun and its use during the last thirty years of the 19th century. Guns, shells, market hunting, etc.)

LINDUSKA, J. P. *Waterfowl Tomorrow*. Government Printing Office, 1964.

(A collection of pieces on all aspects of waterfowl by leading game biologists.)

PARMALEE, P. W., and LOOMIS, F. D. *Decoys and Decoy Carvers of Illinois*. Northern Illinois University Press, 1969.

(Regional in scope but widely appealing, and perhaps our finest book on old decoys with the exception of the Barber volume.)

SEDGWICK, WHITAKER, and HARRISON. *The New Wildfowler in the 1970's*. London: Barrie & Jenkins, 1970.

(A collection of articles from members of The Wildfowlers' Association of Great Britain and Ireland, included here as an interesting look at the way the British do it.)

WALSH, HARRY M. *The Outlaw Gunner*. Tidewater, 1971.

(A well-written, well-illustrated book on the history of market hunting.)

Appendix B: Where to Get It

The following mail-order houses offer catalogs of various items of clothing and equipment of special interest to the duck hunter:

Eddie Bauer, 1737 Airport Way So., Seattle, Wash. 98134
L. L. Bean, Freeport, Me. 04032
Herter's, Inc., Waseca, Minn. 56093
Bob Hinman Outfitters, 1217 W. Glen, Peoria, Ill. 61614
Orvis, Manchester, Vt. 05254

Duck club supplies

Duck-A-Minit, 712 5th St., Arbuckle, Cal. 95912 (duck picker)
Hustler Corp., Jonesboro, Ark. 72401 (all-terrain vehicle)
Kester Game Food Nurseries, Box 371, Oshkosh, Wis. 54901 (duck crops)
McKendree Prod. Co., 1893 Del Moro, Klamath Falls, Ore. 97601 (duck picker)
Wildlife Nurseries, Box 399, Oshkosh, Wis. 54901 (duck food crops)
Woody Mfg. Co., Box 23, Wisconsin Rapids, Wis. 54494 (wood duck nesting houses)
Zoeller Co., 3280 Miller's Ln., Louisville, Ky. 40216 (aeration pumps)

Duck boats

The following firms offer classically styled hunting boats:

Old Town Canoe Co., Old Town, Me. 04468
Stur-Dee Boat Co., Tiverton, R.I. 02878
Viking Enterprises, 916 Milwaukee Ave., Burlington, Wis. 53105

Retriever supplies

Catalog houses offering complete dog equipment:

Bill Boatman & Co., 215 Maple, Bainbridge, Ohio 45612
Sporting Dog Specialties, Spencerport, N.Y. 14559

Calls

The following list is just a sampling of the better-known duck- and goose-call makers:

Black Duck, 1737 Davis Ave., Whiting, Ind. 46394
Faulk's, 616 18th St., Lake Charles, La. 70701
E. V. Iverson, Box 405, San Mateo, Cal. 94401
Lohman, Neosho, Mo. 64850
Chick Majors, Stuttgart, Ark. 72160
Mallard Tone Calls, 2901 16th St., Moline, Ill. 61265
Marshland Call Co., Box 4043, Overland Park, Kan. 66204
Ken Martin Calls, 107th & Archer Ave., Lemont, Ill. 60439
P. S. Olt Co., Pekin, Ill. 61554
Scotch Call Co., 60 Main St., Oakfield, N.Y. 14125
Sure-Shot Game Call Co., Box 816, Groves, Tex. 77619 (Yentzen calls)
Thomas Call Co., Box 336, Winnsboro, Tex. 75494

Decoys

As with boats, certain styles of decoys are better suited to certain types of water than others. The following manufacturers can usually supply a brochure:

John A. Austin, Jr., Box 4751, Memphis, Tenn. 38104 (anchors)
Carry Lite, Inc., 3000 W. Clarke, Milwaukee, Wis. 53245
Chuck Duck Decoys, 119 W. McKinley, Cuba City, Wis. 53807

Decoys Unlimited, Box 69, Clinton, Iowa 52732 (aluminum molds for making decoys)
Dye-Call, Inc., 1309 N. 77th, Seattle, Wash. 98103
G & H Decoys, Box 937, Henrietta, Okla. 74437
Herter's, Inc., Waseca, Minn. 56093
Keyser Decoys, 1325 Industrial Hwy., Southampton, Pa. 18966
McCann Decoys, East Greenbush, N.Y. 12061
Neumann & Bennetts, Box 1497, Klamath Falls, Ore. 97601 (Plasti-Duck)
Otter Plastics Co., Mediapolis, Iowa 52637
Parker Paint Co., Box 433, Green Bay, Wis. 54305 (Decoy and duck boat paint)
Quack Decoy Corp., 4 Mill St., Cumberland, R.I. 02864
TKS Decoys, Box 807, Battle Creek, Mich. 49014 (cork)
TRENDecoy Co., 1663 N. McDuff, Jacksonville, Fla. 32205
Victor-Woodstream, Lititz, Pa. 17543
Wagner Castings Co., Box 1319, Decatur, Ill. 62525 (anchors)

Duck blinds

Ready-made blinds for permanent installation and temporary or portable blinds may be secured from:

Northray Sports Equip. Co., Box 247, Des Moines, Iowa 50265
Smitty's, 522 23rd St., Richmond, Cal. 94804
Sportsman Prod. Mfg. Co., Box 43, Ottawa, Kan. 66067
Waterfowl Supply Co., 182 Greenwich Dr., Pleasant Hill, Cal. 94523
Wildfowler's Mfg. Co., Box 233, Amherst, Ohio 44001 (portable personal blind)

Wildfowl paintings and prints

Wildfowling is an art field unto itself. While few of us can afford an artist's original for club or den, several firms specialize in offering signed limited-edition prints and frequently issue catalogs:

American Wildlife Art Galleries, 926 Plymouth Bldg., Minneapolis, Minn. 55402
Crossroads of Sport, 5 East 47th St., New York, N.Y. 10017

Petersen Galleries, 9433 Wilshire Blvd., Beverly Hills, Cal. 90212

Sportsmen's Edge, Ltd., 136 East 74th St., New York, N.Y. 10021

Wild Wings, Inc., Lake City, Minn. 55041

Book dealers

Great duck-hunting books of the past and present may not be available locally. These dealers can usually supply your library needs:

Angler's & Shooter's Bookshelf, Goshen, Conn. 06756 (out of print)

N. Flayderman Co., R.F.D. 2, New Milford, Conn. 06776

Game Bird Book Case, 138 Grand St., Croton-on-Hudson, N.Y. 10520

Ray Riling Arms Books Co., 6844 Gorsten St., Philadelphia, Pa. 19119

The Sporting Collector, New Haven, Conn. 06513 (out of print)

Appendix C: Wildfowl Photography

Carrying a camera on the hunt is now second nature to me. I only wish I had done so from the beginning. Apparently more and more hunters feel the same way, as I've noticed a camera has become standard hunting equipment. The kind of camera makes little difference. If you're a professional, you'll have professional equipment and demand professional results. But for those of us who simply like to record happy moments of the hunt, almost any camera will do. I have no intention of trying to teach you photography, but have a few tips I'd like to pass on to help you take better hunting pictures.

EXPOSURE

Many of today's "automatic" cameras make pictures that "turn out" even for the rankest beginner. But duck hunting does present certain problems of its own to the photographer. The automatic-exposure devices give only fair results when photographing birds against the sky. If your camera is manual, or has a manual override of the automatic exposure, it is best to get a reading on a duck-colored object and use this exposure when photographing flying birds. Against the sky, your exposure reading will jump, but must be ignored in order to achieve correct exposure on the bird itself.

FOCUSING

When photographing close-flying birds, focusing is also difficult. A handy hint is to find a stick or other object in the water at a certain yardage, and prefocus your camera so that when birds are over the object, they are known to be in focus. If you're trying to capture a photo of birds hit in the air, get on the duck, track it until you hear the report of the gun, and snap simultaneously. Your reaction time will make up for shot travel and within 50 yards will give you a picture at the moment of impact.

SECURITY

Your duck-hunting camera takes a lot of punishment. It helps to shorten the neck strap until the camera hangs high on the chest, minimizing the likelihood the camera will be damaged from swinging to and fro. This shortened strap can also prevent the camera from taking a bath when you lean over the side of the boat or blind. A second strap around the body holds the camera very securely, but is sometimes slow and unhandy to detach for action.

If there is any possibility of boat upset, use a canoeist bag. This is a compartmented inflatable rubber bag that can be blown up to float camera weight, and it is waterproof. It can be attached to the boat with a short cord and should you suddenly find things going overboard, your camera will be safe and dry. Heavy-gauge polyethylene bags may be cut to size, folded, and tied with cord to make a pretty fair float bag. Even a simple plastic bag will do much to keep rain and snow off your camera, yet leave it ready for almost instant use. It becomes especially handy when traveling in a spray-laden boat.

Those with professional-type equipment who are trying for topnotch cold-weather pictures may find it advisable to have their cameras "winterized" by the factory or local shop. This consists of removing all oils and greases, and is a technical and time-consuming job. I would suggest you ask for a price quote before having it done.

Fast film rated at ASA 400 or higher gives a somewhat grainy picture, but this high film speed is often needed under many conditions of light such as early dawn, late dusk, and even the foggy, gray days that find the hunter/photographer at work. This type of low light also gives low-contrast, or muddy, prints, and for best results needs custom printing to produce a usable picture. Since commercial processors commonly use only one grade of paper, ask them for high-contrast.

If you shoot color, ask your dealer for instructions on "pushing" your color film. This will increase your film speed and need only be noted when sending it for processing.

You'll find it difficult to get sharp pictures with telephoto lenses larger than 150mm unless you use a rest or tripod. This will be found especially true in a heaving boat or rocking blind. I don't find gunstock camera mounts much better than conventional hand-holding, but perhaps I have never learned to use them properly. Film is inexpensive as compared to shotgun shells. If there is a picture you especially want, don't hesitate to "bracket" your subject with three different exposures at different lens stops. Take a lot of pictures, and remember: the difference between a good and a bad photographer is that a good photographer doesn't show his bad pictures.

Appendix D: Statistics

ESTIMATED PERCENTAGE OF HUNTER SUCCESS AND AVERAGE OF DAYS HUNTED IN THE UNITED STATES DURING THE COMBINED SEASONS OF 1971 AND 1972

State	Combined 1971-72 average number of days hunted per hunter each season	Combined 1971-72 average total ducks bagged per hunter each season
Alabama	5.51	4.14
Alaska	4.48	5.25
Arizona	5.65	6.10
Arkansas	7.99	8.08
California	7.16	12.19
Colorado	6.32	5.55
Connecticut	5.13	2.71
Delaware	7.51	4.48
Florida	5.33	5.95
Georgia	5.00	4.27
Idaho	6.74	9.37
Illinois	7.10	4.12
Indiana	6.41	3.53
Iowa	8.45	5.54
Kansas	7.78	6.57

State	Combined 1971-72 average number of days hunted per hunter each season	Combined 1971-72 average total ducks bagged per hunter each season
Kentucky	6.74	3.93
Louisiana	7.17	9.55
Maine	5.44	4.69
Maryland	7.45	3.60
Massachusetts	5.83	2.76
Michigan	6.01	3.26
Minnesota	6.62	5.96
Mississippi	5.70	6.05
Missouri	6.09	3.85
Montana	5.87	5.86
Nebraska	7.66	5.84
Nevada	5.28	6.83
New Hampshire	5.74	2.38
New Jersey	5.77	3.55
New Mexico	5.06	4.56
New York	5.75	2.72
North Carolina	6.25	4.49
North Dakota	7.34	7.19
Ohio	5.99	2.90
Oklahoma	6.45	6.10
Oregon	6.62	6.77
Pennsylvania	4.86	1.86
Rhode Island	7.77	4.60
South Carolina	7.11	5.81
South Dakota	8.19	7.12
Tennessee	7.40	6.33
Texas	5.29	5.81
Utah	6.06	7.89
Vermont	5.77	3.88
Virginia	5.86	5.52
Washington	7.05	6.89
West Virginia	4.57	2.19
Wisconsin	6.84	3.76
Wyoming	5.62	5.57

ESTIMATED BAG (RETRIEVED) BY SPECIES OF FOUR FLYWAYS DURING 1971 AND 1972 HUNTING SEASONS

	Season	Pacific Flyway	Central Flyway	Mississippi Flyway	Atlantic Flyway
Mallard	1971	1,288,000	1,172,100	2,189,200	348,900
	1972	1,277,700	1,195,300	1,918,800	366,200
Domestic	1971	1,700	400	6,500	6,300
mallard	1972	2,200	1,300	6,400	8,300
Black duck	1971	0	200	105,900	290,900
	1972	0	1,300	109,700	233,100
Gadwall	1971	134,100	316,400	287,700	16,900
	1972	103,100	300,800	282,700	23,600
American	1971	478,700	184,800	191,900	48,100
wigeon	1972	397,800	158,500	218,600	63,200
Green-winged	1971	483,500	313,000	333,100	147,600
teal	1972	526,600	322,700	314,700	113,300
Blue-winged and cinnamon	1971	65,700	216,500	579,800	43,700
teal	1972	97,900	184,600	422,200	72,400
Shoveler	1971	237,400	86,800	90,800	11,500
	1972	204,200	116,900	102,200	12,500
Pintail	1971	970,000	161,500	125,000	26,100
	1972	895,000	145,800	134,000	24,400
Wood duck	1971	33,100	39,200	571,900	281,700
	1972	31,800	40,000	513,200	298,300
Redhead	1971	51,600	59,900	86,000	23,000
	1972	26,000	12,200	10,600	1,700
Canvasback	1971	55,000	14,700	39,100	32,900
	1972	2,000	700	900	200
Greater scaup	1971	17,500	1,800	26,900	56,300
	1972	18,600	2,700	33,900	76,200
Lesser scaup	1971	32,700	79,000	320,800	84,500
	1972	20,600	92,300	317,100	27,900
Ring-necked	1971	18,200	27,300	300,400	79,200
duck	1972	25,900	32,700	215,600	63,800

Adapted from estimates gathered by the Bureau of Sport Fisheries and Wildlife.

ESTIMATED BAG (RETRIEVED) BY SPECIES OF FOUR FLYWAYS DURING 1971 AND 1972 HUNTING SEASONS

	Season	Pacific Flyway	Central Flyway	Mississippi Flyway	Atlantic Flyway
Goldeneye	1971	18,900	5,800	37,300	26,300
	1972	15,400	5,000	47,200	32,900
Bufflehead	1971	30,700	19,800	49,700	62,500
	1972	21,300	10,000	70,700	53,700
Ruddy duck	1971	41,200	12,800	27,800	12,100
	1972	46,600	15,700	35,100	10,900
Oldsquaw	1971	200	0	1,900	14,300
	1972	300	100	1,200	12,700
Eider	1971	0	0	0	13,900
	1972	0	0	0	17,900
Scoter	1971	2,300	1,100	4,500	49,300
	1972	2,000	0	2,800	38,500
Hooded	1971	2,600	4,400	28,200	21,800
merganser	1972	5,800	1,900	30,800	14,800
Other	1971	6,400	5,200	4,700	10,400
mergansers	1972	6,800	1,400	9,500	11,300
Other ducks	1971	300	300	1,000	1,100
	1972	1,500	1,900	600	4,600
Coot	1971	151,200	80,700	428,800	161,400
	1972	125,900	94,500	561,500	106,600
Canada goose	1971	179,200	193,400	194,700	258,700
(and subspecies)	1972	241,700	112,400	165,200	204,100
Snow goose	1971	112,900	119,100	52,200	100
(and Ross's)	1972	43,600	101,500	48,900	0
Blue goose	1971	0	60,800	113,600	0
	1972	0	37,900	57,400	0
White-fronted	1971	35,400	39,800	20,100	0
goose	1972	52,400	36,500	10,900	0
Brant	1971	2,900	0	0	79,100
	1972	14,600	0	0	0

Adapted from estimates gathered by the Bureau of Sport Fisheries and Wildlife.
Extreme variances between years in bags of some species may be due to lower limits or a closed season.

NUMBER OF POTENTIAL HUNTERS PER STATE ACCORDING TO DUCK STAMPS SOLD IN 1971

State	Total Duck Stamps Sold in 1971	State	Total Duck Stamps Sold in 1971
Alabama	12,909	Montana	28,241
Alaska	14,423	Nebraska	50,898
Arizona	15,465	Nevada	15,029
Arkansas	55,656	New Hampshire	9,973
California	173,474	New Jersey	43,673
Colorado	47,717	New Mexico	7,324
Connecticut	17,389	New York	116,371
Delaware	12,987	North Carolina	30,151
Dist. of Columbia	3,420	North Dakota	53,600
Florida	33,576	Ohio	45,075
Georgia	15,429	Oklahoma	36,049
Idaho	33,640	Oregon	58,730
Illinois	82,706	Pennsylvania	89,350
Indiana	32,769	Rhode Island	4,354
Iowa	68,401	South Carolina	20,731
Kansas	63,756	South Dakota	46,670
Kentucky	11,390	Tennessee	33,677
Louisiana	120,874	Texas	148,047
Maine	18,534	Utah	37,588
Maryland	32,646	Vermont	8,758
Massachusetts	26,106	Virginia	19,757
Michigan	111,785	Washington	77,067
Minnesota	179,624	West Virginia	1,858
Mississippi	29,055	Wisconsin	160,435
Missouri	59,435	Wyoming	9,486

United States Total: 2,426,058. About 1¼% sold to nonhunters. Figures do not include stamps sold in Hawaii, Puerto Rico, or by the Philatelic Agency.

Index

PICTURE CREDITS

Most of the photographs that illustrate this book were taken by the author. However, I would like to thank the following individuals and organizations for their permission to use the illustrations that appear on the pages specified:

Ed Bry— 12, 13, 14, 17, 18, 36, 82, 223

Illinois Department of Conservation— 21

James R. Olt— 129

U.S. Fish and Wildlife Service— 2, 3

Robert Vinovich— 20, 116

Washington State Department of Game— 132